D1497531

GREAT RUNS
in Boston

by Mark Lowenstein

FRESH TRACKS PRESS

BROOKLINE, MASSACHUSETTS

Great Runs in Boston

First Edition
Second Printing, April 2010

Copyright © 2009 by Mark Lowenstein

Maps: MapResources.com. Additional maps used with permission.
Designed by Robert Pehlke Design, Brookline, MA | www.pehlkedesign.com
Book design production by Adam Katz | www.atomikdesignstudio.com

ISBN 978-0-9822485-2-2

Printed in Canada

Published by:
Fresh Tracks Press
158 Winthrop Rd., Suite 250
Brookline, MA 02445
www.freshtrackspress.com

All rights reserved. Except as indicated, no part of this book may be reproduced, stored in a retrieval system, or transmitted, in any form, or by any means, electronic, mechanical, photocopying, filming, microfilming, or otherwise, without express written permission from the author.

Correspondence regarding this book can be sent to:
Mark Lowenstein
c/o Fresh Tracks Press
158 Winthrop Rd, Suite 250
Brookline, MA 02445
mark.lowenstein@greatruns.net
www.greatruns.net

Safety Notice: Although Fresh Tracks Press and the author have made every attempt to ensure that the information in this book is accurate at press time, they are not responsible for any loss, damage, injury, or inconvenience that may occur to anyone while using this book. You are responsible for your own safety and health while following the walking and running routes described here. Always check local conditions, know your own limitations, and consult a map. Also be aware that some roads and paths have variable surface, traffic, and lighting conditions, and that there are continual changes that might affect routes.

Contents

Neighborhood Runs

Boston and The Water

Greenways, Parks, and Off-Road Paths

Dedication

To my wife Jenn, and children Hannah and Zachary, for their continued support of my "addiction" over the years, and for their grace in allowing me the time to work on this book.

To my father, for his energy, drive, entrepreneurial spirit, and zest for life.

To the visionaries who work tirelessly to help create the spaces that make Boston one of America's great running cities.

Foreword

Why I Wrote This Book

The idea for this book came from two realizations. First, as an outdoors enthusiast, I've noticed the many books devoted to helping people discover good routes and places to go. "Short Bike Rides in Boston", "Top Ten Day Hikes in New England" — there are seemingly guides like this for every sport that has a route. But I've noticed very few guides designed for runners. This might be because running is more of a routine that people do from their homes, with a set of three or four regular "routes". However, with a little extra effort — and help from this book — a whole new world can open up.

Second, having lived in several Massachusetts communities over the past 20 years, I'd like to share some of the great routes I've discovered. Running is a great way to explore an area, and it is also important to vary one's routes in order to keep fresh.

This book is oriented toward the casual runner, with an emphasis on enhancing the experience of what can be — let's face it — an occasionally boring and lonely pursuit. I have taken the time to map out a great variety of interesting routes, suiting different types of runners, terrain, moods, seasons, and running conditions. Every run has been meticulously researched, and contains detailed directions, notes about signage, and facts about interesting sites.

Also notable is that this book represents the first time detailed route descriptions and maps for the vast majority of Boston's great collection of pathways, ponds, linear parks and waterfront walks — HarborWalk, Emerald Necklace, Charles River Paths, Southwest Corridor Park, several new Greenways — can all be found in one place.

Great Runs in Boston is the second in a series of books covering the Boston metro area. The first book, *Great Runs in Brookline and Vicinity*, was published in February 2009, and has received a terrific response to date. With your support, additional books covering more areas are on the way!

Running in Boston

Boston is one of the country's great cities for running, featuring a great deal of variety within a relatively small geographic footprint. Some of the most famous city runs in the world are located in Boston, from the Charles River Paths to the greenery and majesty of the Olmsted-designed Emerald Necklace. There are also some spectacular runs along the waterfront, which has become much more accessible to the public over the past several years, as a result of the Big Dig and efforts of many of our civic leaders, local businesses, and countless volunteers.

Boston's density and relatively small size are also assets. Three-quarters of the 30+ runs in this book, for example, start within a mile or so from any point downtown. Just about any run can be easily accessed by public transportation. I have also designed a few special "Run" & "T" routes that enable a longer, one-way run, using the "T" to get to the start or return from the finish. Examples here include the "Marathon Training" runs, Southwest Corridor Park, and the "Three Pond Tour".

For those of you who associate running in Boston with the Charles River Paths, Back Bay, Emerald Necklace, and occasional waterfront jaunt, I'd encourage you to try some of the "hidden gems" of Boston running. These include:

- The improved waterfront paths and quaint side streets of Charlestown
- The continually improving and accessible HarborWalk, which now covers more than 13 miles almost seamlessly from Charlestown to UMASS Boston, with many additional sections and spurs.
- Some terrific runs in East Boston and Winthrop, including Deer Island and the new East Boston Greenway
- Southwest Corridor Park, which runs 4 miles from the Back Bay T Station to Forest Hills.
- The entire area encompassed by the Riverway, Jamaica Pond, Arnold Arboretum, Franklin Park, and Forest Hills Cemetery — more than 30 miles of off-road running heaven!
- Some of Boston's historic "parkways" — listed on the National Register of Historic Places — are great for running, with their grassy medians and leafy canopy.

Downtown Boston also features some great neighborhood runs, which include some of the city's most historic sights, quaint streets, and elegant residences. This book features some terrific runs on the main streets and back roads of the South End, Back Bay, Charlestown, Beacon Hill, the North End, South Boston, and East Boston. Most of these runs are on designated running paths or use quieter, less-trafficked roads. A few of the runs in this book stretch into some of Boston's closer-in suburbs, notably Brookline, which features the great "three Ps" of running — parks, ponds, and pathways — as well as some pleasant residential neighborhoods.

It is also gratifying that the running scene in Boston continues to improve. Notable developments include an increasingly accessible, seamless, and well-marked Harbor Walk, stretching some 17 miles from Charlestown to the Neponset River. There is also a significant network of unsung new greenway and HarborWalk paths in East Boston, Winthrop and near Logan Airport.

The Big Dig project has opened up 25 acres of parkland, officially called the Rose Kennedy Greenway, over what used to be the traffic-clogged Central Artery running through downtown. For runners, the Greenway is a pleasant 1.5 mile path from Chinatown to North Station, featuring numerous parks, architectural features, artistic displays, and well-designed pedestrian crossings.

Concerns about the environment, global warming, and obesity have led to movements encouraging a more healthy, pedestrian-friendly lifestyle. This can be seen all over Boston, from new bike lanes and racks to better signage, new and upgraded parks, and small but significant touches such as improved lighting and street crossings. These improvements are the result of a huge effort by Boston's political, business, and civic leadership.

Note For Walkers

Despite the title, this book should appeal to walkers as well. Since most of the "routes" in the themed runs average around five miles, they would fall into the category of "long walk". Many of the routes in this book are divided into distinct, "walker-friendly" segments. Walkers can also use parts of the runs, or the maps included for each run, to construct their own, shorter, and very delightful routes.

Approach

The main objective of this book is to provide as many options for enjoyable running as possible. Most runs are designed to be a loop rather than "there and back". Another goal is to keep off the main roads, and away from streets with lots of traffic, poor sidewalks, or that are unappealing in other ways. Many runs have a "theme", to make them differentiated, easy to remember, and more fun. There is very little overlap between the 30 or so runs featured in this book. The book is "spiral bound", to make it easy for runners to make copies of individual runs instead of having to carry the book.

In order to effectively organize the routes and help you find the best run suiting your preferences, the book is divided into three categories: Neighborhood Runs; Boston and the Water; and Greenways, Parks, and Off-Road Paths.

The routes in this book are designed for the casual runner: the average distance is five miles. There are some longer runs, or suggestions for additional "spurs" for distance runners. There are also a few runs, or notes within runs, for those who are looking for hills, tracks, or good places to do interval training.

Each run has been meticulously researched, with great effort to find the most scenic routes and the most pleasant streets or paths. There is careful attention to detail, including notes about missing signage, tough crossings, type of terrain, and interesting/historic sites.

Running is Hyper-Local

Because most regular runners like to start their runs from where they live or are staying, it is a challenge to design the right "starting point" for each route. To deal with this, I decided to start most of the routes in this book from a small number of "central locations", notably: Kenmore Square, Back Bay (Public Garden), and North Station.

Most people living in downtown Boston (Beacon Hill, Charlestown, North End, Waterfront, Back Bay, Fenway, South End, Financial District) are a mile from one of these starting points. As an additional aid, the matrix on pages 14-15 shows seven principal locations in Boston, with information about the distance and the most direct (not always the most scenic!) route between them.

Structure for Each Run

Every run has a set structure, featuring an overview, description of the run, detailed directions, and a map with a shaded route, mileage markers, and directional arrows. Below is a guide to the major categories.

Overview

At the beginning of each run is an overview table, containing an at-a-glance list of the specifics across several categories.

Distance

This is the run's total distance, in miles, always returning to the starting point. Runners will have to factor in the extra distance from their point of origin.

Starting Point

Many of the runs in this book start from a small number of "central locations", notably: Kenmore Square, Back Bay (Public Garden), and North Station. Most people living or staying in downtown Boston are a mile or so of one of these starting points. As an additional aid, the matrix on pages 14-15 shows seven principal locations in Boston, with information about the distance and the most direct (not always the most scenic!) route between them.

Terrain

This is brief commentary on the type of terrain, such as whether the run is mainly on or off-road; quality of surface; and elevation. Most of Boston is relatively flat. The hilliest sections are Beacon Hill and Bunker Hill. Peter's Hill, located in the Arnold Arboretum, has Boston's highest elevation, at 235 feet, and features spectacular views of the city. For those seeking hill work, head out to Brookline, which features several substantial hills of up to 350 feet, and a fascinating network of "stair paths".

Lighting
Lots of people run at night, or early in the morning before it gets light. Some streets are better lit than others, and some of the off-road paths are not lit at all.

Bathrooms
Public restroom facilities (libraries, public parks, etc) on or near the route are listed. Note that the hours of these facilities will vary and are sometimes unpredictable. Also listed are select commercial establishments that are known to be more "bathroom-friendly" to the public, such as Starbucks.

Water
Drinking fountains accessible to the public, usually in parks or other civic facilities, are listed. Usually outdoor fountains do not work in winter.

Interesting Sites
Attention here is to major landmarks, historic buildings, and other places of interest.

Additional Spurs
This is designed for people who want to construct a longer run, or for situations where there might be a particularly appealing add-on.

Bests

This is a list of my favorite runs, or sections of runs, for different categories.

History
- Historic Charlestown
- Back Bay Shopping Trip
- Beacon Hill & North End
- South End: Main Streets and Back Roads runs

Greenery
- Arnold Arboretum
- Riverway/Jamaicaway paths
- Franklin Park
- Forest Hills Cemetery
- Three Pond Tour

Beautiful Homes
- Back Bay runs
- South End Squares
- Beacon Hill
- Dip into Brookline

Running at Night
- Commonwealth Ave. Mall between Massachusetts Ave. and Arlington St.
- Beacon St., as far as west as Cleveland Circle
- Back Bay
- South End Main Streets

Off-Road Runs
- Waterfront/HarborWalk – downtown & South Boston
- Riverway/Jamaicaway
- Charles River Paths
- Southwest Corridor Park
- Neponset Valley Greenway

Hilly Runs/Sections
- Beacon Hill (up to 135 ft.)
- Bunker Hill, Charlestown (100 ft.)
- Peter's Hill, Arnold Arboretum (235 ft.)
- Hills and stair paths of Brookline - try Summit Ave.!

Water Views
- Charles River Paths
- HarborWalk – Charlestown, downtown, and South Boston sections
- Jamaicaway/Riverway, including Jamaica Pond
- Deer Island, Winthrop
- East Boston: Piers Park, HarborWalk, Constitution Beach
- Spectacle Island

Long Runs Without Lots of Turns
- Riverway/Jamaicaway paths
- Charles River Paths
- Commonwealth Ave. Esplanade, through Public Garden and Boston Common
- Deer Island
- South Boston HarborWalk

Options for Winter *(when roads are icy or snowy)*

Note: most of the off-road paths, such as those along the Charles River, the Southwest Corridor, and the Jamaicaway/Riverway are NOT maintained in winter. Along the waterfront, some of the heavier pedestrian sections are maintained (ie. plowed and sanded). The best options for winter when sidewalks are snow-covered include:
- Beacon St.
- Main streets of Back Bay
- Main streets of South End
- The local gym (!)

Track Work and Intervals
- Downes Field (near Jamaica Pond) – great artificial track, ¼ mile around
- Track in the Back Bay Fens at Roberto Clemente Field
- Franklin Park: track at White stadium; cross country track/trails

One-Way and "T"
These are longer routes that some runners might want to run one-way, using the "T" to access the beginning or return from the end of the route.

- **Boston Marathon Trainer.** Out Beacon St./Commonwealth Ave. to Rt. 16 in Newton, D Line back from Woodland. Or take the D Line out to Woodland and run back. West of Newton, the Marathon route follows the Framingham/Worcester line of the Commuter Rail, with stops in Wellesley Hills, Wellesley Square (Wellesley Center), Natick, West Natick, Framingham, and Ashland.

- **Beacon Street Special.** The 8.3 mile run on Beacon St. between Kenmore Square and Newton has several T stops along the way for those who want to run one-way. From Kenmore Sq. to Cleveland Circle, there are Green Line stops every few blocks along the middle of Beacon St. (C Line). West of Cleveland Circle, the most easily accessible stops are on the D line at Newton Center, Waban, and Woodland.

- **Southwest Corridor.** This route links the Back Bay or Copley Square stations on the east end, and the Forest Hills Station on the west end (Orange & Green Lines). There are several Orange line stops along the SW Corridor path as well.

- **Silver Line link.** The new Silver Line — basically a glorified bus — runs along Washington St. and can be used by runners who want to run on the Southwest Corridor Park or extend the South End run on Washington St. to Dudley Square. The Silver Line also has several stops on the Waterfront, which is helpful for the HarborWalk runs.

- **East Boston and Winthrop.** East Boston cannot be accessed from downtown by foot. However, the terrific run along the East Boston Greenway, Piers Park, and Harborside Drive is easily accessible from the Blue Line T stations at Airport or Maverick.

- **Three Pond Tour.** This is a fabulous run, starting at Kenmore Sq. and incorporating Jamaica Pond, the Brookline Hill Reservoir, and Chestnut Hill Reservoir, with great pathway and neighborhood connectors in between. The run can be reduced from 12 to 9 miles by hopping on the C line at Cleveland Circle, or the D line nearby at Chestnut Hill Ave., and returning downtown.

Some Key Distances

Many of the runs in this book start from a small number of "central locations", notably: Kenmore Square, Back Bay (Public Garden), North Station, Aquarium (central point on waterfront), the South End, and two locations along the Charles River paths. Most people living or staying in downtown Boston (Beacon Hill, Waterfront, Back Bay, Fenway, South End) are within a mile or so of one of these starting points. As an additional aid, the matrix below shows seven principal locations, with information about the most direct (not always the most scenic!) route and distance between them.

See charts on following pages.

Main Starting Points for Running in Boston

Kenmore Square:	Intersection of Brookline Ave., Beacon St., Commonwealth Ave.
Public Garden:	Entrance gate at Commonwealth Ave. and Arlington St.
North Station:	"T" Station, at Causeway St. and Canal St.
Charles River East:	Fiedler Pedestrian Br. near intersection of Arlington St. and Beacon St.
Charles River West:	River Path at Harvard Bridge (Mass. Ave.), Boston side
Aquarium:	Aquarium T station (Blue Line) at State St. on Long Wharf
South End:	East Berkeley St. and Tremont St.

Part A. Most Direct Routes Between Key Points in Boston

	Kenmore Sq.	Back Bay/Public Garden	North Station	River Path East	River Path West	Waterfront (Aquarium)	South End
Kenmore Sq.	x	Comm. Ave. east	Comm. Ave. west-Public Garden-Boston Common-Bowdoin St.-Staniford St.	Comm. Ave. east to Mass. Ave and along river	Comm. Ave. to Mass. Ave	Comm. Ave. west-Public Garden-Boston Common-Tremont St.-Court-State St.	Comm. Ave. to Berkeley St. to Tremont St.
Back Bay/Pubic Garden	Comm. Ave. west	x	Public Garden-Boston Common-Bowdoin-Staniford	Arlington St. to Beacon St. to Fiedler Br.	Comm. Ave. to Mass. Ave. to river	Public Garden-Boston Common-Tremont-Court-State St.	Berkeley St. to Tremont St.
North Station	Staniford St-Cambridge St.-Bowdoin St.-Common-Public Garden- Comm Ave. heading west		x	Staniford St.-Cambridge St. to Charles/MGH to Fiedler overpass	Causeway St. to Lomansey Way to Charles River Path to Mass. Ave.	Causeway St. to Commercial St. to Aquarium	Staniford St.-Bowdoin St.-Cambridge St.-Tremont St. to E. Berkeley St.
River Path East	Over Fiedler Br. to Arlington St. to Comm. Ave.	Over Fiedler Br. to Arlington St. to Public Garden	River path to Leverett Circle, Nashua St. to Causeway St.	x	River Path to Mass. Ave	Charles/MGH overpass-Cambridge St.-Tremont St.-Court St.-State St. to Long-Wharf	Charles St., past Public Garden, to Tremont St. to E. Berkeley St.
River Path West	Mass. Ave. to Comm. Ave.	Mass. Ave. to Comm. Ave. to Public Garden	River path to Leverett Circle, Nashua St. to Causeway St.	Path to Fiedler overpass	x	To Garden, through Garden, Common to Tremont St., to Court St. to State St.	Mass. Ave. south, all the way to Tremont St. then to E. Berkeley St.

Part A. Most Direct Routes Between Key Points in Boston (continued)

	Kenmore Sq.	Back Bay/Public Garden	North Station	River Path East	River Path West	Waterfront (Aquarium)	South End
Waterfront/Aquarium	State St.-Court St.-Tremont St.-Common-Public Garden-Comm. Ave. heading east	State St.-Court St.-Tremont St.-Common-Public Garden	Commercial St. to Causeway St.	State St.-Court St.-Tremont St.-Cambridge St.-Charles/MGH overpass to Fiedler Br.	To River path East, then along path to Mass Ave.	x	State St.-Court St.-Tremont St. to E. Berkeley St.
South End	Tremont St.-Berkeley St. to Comm Ave., heading east	Berkeley St. to Comm. Ave. to Garden	To Public Garden-Boston Common-Bowdoin St.-Stanihope St.-Causeway St.	Tremont St. to Charles St. to Charles MGH	To River path East, then along path to Mass Ave.	Tremont St.-Court St.-State St.	x

Part B. Distances Between Key Points (using routes from Part A, in miles)

	Kenmore Sq.	Back Bay/Public Garden	North Station	River Path East	River Path West	Waterfront/Aquarium	South End
Kenmore Sq.	X	1.3	2.5	0.6	1.9	2.5	1.7
Back Bay/Public Garden	1.3	X	1.25	0.7	1.1	1.2	0.7
North Station	2.5	1.25	X	0.9	2.1	1.1	1.8
River Path East	0.6	0.7	0.9	X	1.2	1.25	1.3
River Path West	1.9	1.1	2.1	1.2	X	2.3	1.7
Waterfront/Aquarium	2.5	1.2	1.1	1.25	2.3	X	1.6
South End	1.7	0.7	1.8	1.3	1.7	1.6	X

Acknowledgements

The concept for this book has been greeted with great enthusiasm. As a first-time author, I am grateful to the many people who have offered support for this project. I did want to call out a few select groups and individuals who have been especially supportive of *Great Runs*. Special thanks to:

Robert Pehlke, whose design company is to be credited for the great look of this book, has been very generous with his time and insight.

Adam Katz of Adam Katz Graphic Design, for his continued diligence and creativity.

My assistant, Stephanie Yang, for her ability to take on just about anything!

Colin Peddie and the team at Marathon Sports, for their continued support of *Great Runs* and the Boston running community.

The team at Brookline Booksmith, for their unvarying support of local authors and community initiatives.

Numerous friends, peers, and family who have given generously of their time in listening about, providing feedback regarding, and otherwise putting up with this project: Jon and Donna Frankel, Andy Eschtruth, Elana Varon, Liana Lowenstein, Justin Sanft, Paul and Jewel Lowenstein, Barrie and Carole Greiff, Howard Anderson.

Numerous Individuals and Organizations who have given generously of their time and have been a terrific support: Viven Li, Boston Harbor Association; Dan Driscoll, Massachusetts Dept. of Conservation and Recreation; Susan Knight, Emerald Necklace Conservancy; Cecily Miller, Forest Hills Educational Trust; Lori Kauffman, Brookline Booksmith; Joseph McConkey, Boston Running Center; Candice Cook, Boston Natural Areas Network; Julie Warsowe, Arnold Arboretum; Linda Pehlke, author of *Exploring the Paths of Brookline*; the 5:30 a.m. shift at the Starbucks in Washington Square.

A special thanks to my wife, Jenn, who has provided valuable insight during the production and editing process, and has uncomplainingly supported my "second job" over these last several months. And to my children, Hannah and Zachary, for their encouragement, enthusiasm, and acceptance of fewer "pancake Sundays" of late.

Historic Squares and Gas Lamps:
Beacon Hill, North End, Charlestown

ESSENTIALS		
DISTANCE **7.2** Miles	**STARTING POINT**	Public Garden Gate, Arlington St.
	TERRAIN	A few modest hills; all paved but some off-road
	LIGHTING	OK for running at night; charming gas lamps on Beacon Hill, in Charlestown
	BATHROOMS	Boston Common; USS Constitution Museum in Charlestown
	WATER	Boston Common; USS Constitution Museum in Charlestown
	INTERESTING SITES	Public Garden, Boston Common, streets of Beacon Hill, Old North Church, Paul Revere House, Bunker Hill Monument
	PUBLIC TRANSPORTATION	T stops throughout run

Overview

This run, which could also be a good long walk, packs many of Boston's landmark sights and iconic neighborhoods into a small geographic footprint. In about seven miles you will see: the Public Garden; Boston Common; the State House; the hills and gas lamps of Beacon Hill; City Hall; Faneuil Hall; the waterfront at Long Wharf; sections of the North End, including the Old North Church, Paul Revere House, and Copps Hill Cemetery; the charming back streets of Charlestown, leading to the Bunker Hill Monument; and the shops of Charles Street. Most of the run is on less-trafficked back streets. Depending on the time of day, you might have to stick to sidewalks in certain sections due to the narrowness of the streets.

START: Public Garden entrance gate, Arlington St. & Commonwealth Ave.

0.0   Enter Public Garden at the Arlington St./Commonwealth Ave. gate (G. Washington Statue) to intersection with Charles St.

0.2   **CROSS** Charles St. and enter Boston Common.

       TURN IMMEDIATELY LEFT onto path paralleling Charles St., to end.

       RIGHT on the path in the Common that parallels Beacon St. to your left, up hill, to the State House.

0.6   **EXIT COMMON** at State House, then **TURN AROUND** and run back down Beacon St. to Joy St.

       RIGHT on Joy St.

       1st LEFT, on Mt. Vernon St., very charming.

0.9   **RIGHT** at Louisburg Square, an exclusive residential section of Beacon Hill. One block to Pinckney St.

       RIGHT on Pinckney St. to end (Joy St.)

1.2   **LEFT** on Joy St., down hill, to Cambridge St., crossing to north side.

       RIGHT on Cambridge St. Follow to the Goverment Center T Station in City Hall Plaza.

1.5   At Government Center T Station, **GO THROUGH** City Hall Plaza, to Congress St., keeping Court St. on your right. Come to a crossing light at Congress St.

1.8   **CROSS** Congress St., and **ENTER** Faneuil Hall Marketplace at the Adams Statue, with Bostix on your right.

       RUN THROUGH Faneuil Hall/Quincy Market, keeping the Faneuil Hall/ Quincy Market buildings on your left.

       NOTE: Bill Rodgers running center is in Faneuil Hall.

2.0   At end of Faneuil Hall, at archway, (Brookstone, Orvis), **CROSS** the surface artery into Columbus Park, with nice water views on Long Wharf.

       LEFT AND THROUGH Columbus Park, under the "trellis", heading north away from the Marriott and toward the North End.

       CROSS Atlantic Ave. onto Richmond St., entering the North End. *Caution: Narrow streets.*

2.3   **RIGHT** on North St., to North Square. Paul Revere House is on the left.

       BEAR LEFT at North Square to Prince St.

       LEFT on Prince St. to Hanover St.

       RIGHT on Hanover St. to intersection with Charter St. at Harry Moore Sq.

2.7   **LEFT** on Charter St., to top of hill with the Historic Burying Ground on the left and Copps Hill Terrace on the right, with nice views down to the water.

2.9   **LEFT** on Snow Hill St., keeping cemetery wall on the left.

       RIGHT on Prince St.

3.2   **LEFT** on Commercial St.

RIGHT on the Charlestown Bridge (N. Washington St.). Fine views of water and Zakim Bridge.

3.6   **RIGHT** on Chelsea St. at the Marriott Residence Inn. **ALMOST IMMEDIATELY, RIGHT** at Sorelle Bakery, and **DOWN STAIRS.** Follow to Constitution Center sign.

    LEFT on Constitution Rd., following to the USS Constitution Museum.

    Option: Add ½ m along water, following HarborWalk signs to 16th & 1st St.

4.1   **LEFT** on 5th St. and return on 2nd Ave., a pleasant pedestrian mall through historic buildings of Charlestown Navy Yard.

    AT END OF 2nd Ave., **RIGHT** on Constitution Ave. and then **IMMEDIATELY LEFT** on Chelsea St., to Warren St.

4.4   **RIGHT** on Warren St. to Monument St.

4.6   **RIGHT** on Monument St. Classic Victorian-era row houses, gas lamps. Continue to top of hill and Bunker Hill Monument.

    LOOP AROUND Monument Square, to Winthrop St.

4.9   **DOWN HILL** at Winthrop St., past a lovely courtyard, to Main St.

    RIGHT on Main St., briefly, to Harvard St.

    HOOK LEFT on Harvard St. — another charming section. Follow to end at City Sq., famous Olives restaurant.

5.1   **CROSS** N. Washington St. onto the west side of Charlestown Bridge, and **TURN LEFT. GO DOWN STAIRS** at Paul Revere Park sign (instead of crossing over the bridge).

    FOLLOW Paul Revere Park to the water.

    CROSS FLOATING SIDEWALK at the end of the park, crossing the water. **EXIT** parking lot onto Causeway St.

5.8   **RIGHT** on Causeway St., passing by the TD Bank North Garden, to the end, at the Tip O'Neill building.

6.0   **CROSS** Causeway St. **CONTINUE STRAIGHT,** up Staniford St., to Cambridge St.

6.2   **CROSS** Cambridge St., **CROSSING** onto Temple St. (no sign) in the Beacon Hill area.

    STRAIGHT on Temple St., to the end.

    RIGHT at end (no sign). Street turns into Myrtle St.

    CONTINUE on Myrtle St., up and over the hill, following down the hill and around to Revere St. (no sign).

6.7   **LEFT** on Revere St. and down hill to Charles St.

    LEFT on Charles St., which is a lovely commercial area filled with eclectic shops and restaurants.

7.0   **CROSS** Beacon St., and enter corner gate of Public Garden, pass "Make Way for Ducklings" statue, to the center part of the garden, over the bridge, returning to Arlington St. and the beginning of the run.

7.2   **END**

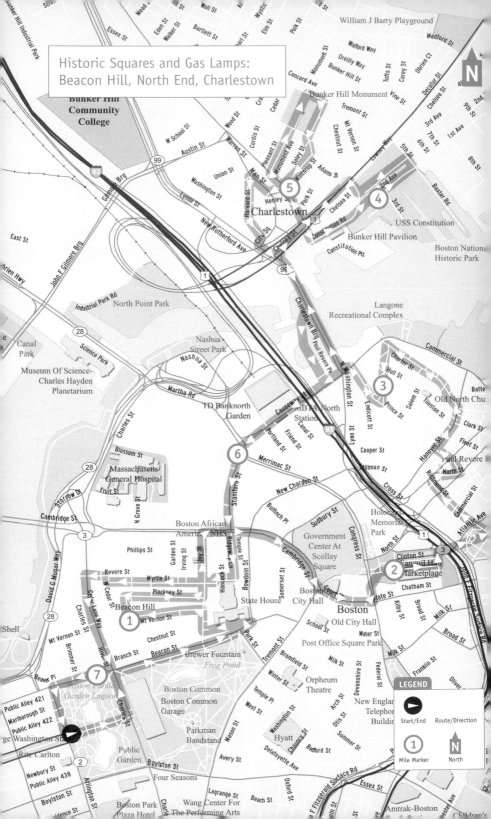

From the Water to Bunker Hill:
Historic Charlestown

ESSENTIALS		
DISTANCE **5.4** Miles	**STARTING POINT**	North Station
	TERRAIN	Flat; much of run is off-road
	LIGHTING	Good on streets. Some sections of HarborWalk section are not lit at night.
	BATHROOMS	North Station, USS Constitution Museum
	WATER	Boston Common; USS Constitution Museum in Charlestown
	INTERESTING SITES	HarborWalk path, views of Zakim Bridge, USS Constitution, Bunker Hill Monument, historic homes, new Paul Revere Park
	PARKING	Public lots at North Station; meters in Charlestown
	PUBLIC TRANSPORTATION	North Station, Sullivan Square (Orange Line)

Overview

Many who live downtown overlook Charlestown, which has much to offer in a very compact geography. The route includes some of the most scenic sections of the HarborWalk; the USS Constitution; a "Rocky"-like approach to the Bunker Hill Monument, and some of the lovelier, gas-lamped side streets of one of Boston's most historic neighborhoods. Almost the entire run is on paths or on quiet, non-trafficked roads.

This run has two distinct sections — the first part takes you from North Station, across the water on a "floating" sidewalk, with great views of the Zakim Bridge, and then along the water in Charlestown for about 1.5 miles, past the USS Constitution and following HarborWalk sections through the Navy Yard. The second part features some of the historic streets and sites of Charlestown, anchored by the Bunker Hill Monument and including charming Monument Square, Winthrop Square, and the John Harvard Mall. The total run is nearly 5.4 miles. Those who want a shorter run or a nice walk can choose either the "water" or "monument" section of this run. And for more distance, I'd recommend some of the avenues (1st to 5th) in the Boston Naval Shipyard, paralleling the water, featuring numerous historic buildings, as well as up and down some of the piers (0.2-0.3m each).

Distance	Directions

START: North Station, at Canal and Causeway St.

0.0 **PROCEED EAST** along Causeway St., briefly, to Beverly St. Extension, just after TD BankNorth Garden.

LEFT on Beverly St. Extension, straight through to the Police Marine Division parking lot. At the end, **CROSS OVER FLOATING SIDEWALK,** to Paul Revere Park in Charlestown. (*Caution: slippery and narrow*).

0.3 **HEAD RIGHT** out of the park, along Constitution Rd. in front of the Marriott hotel, past the Constitution Landing sign, past gate, to USS Constitution Museum.

Options: lovely ¼ mile spur along the HW behind the Marriott Hotel, around the Marina, ending abruptly at a gate so you will have to double back. Also numerous opportunities to run down a couple of the piers.

0.8 **FOLLOW HW** sign on the east side of the pier (closest to museum). Terrific views.

1.1 Pier 6, Tavern on the Water restaurant.

CONTINUE following HW, past piers 6,7,8. Interesting buildings and interpretive signs. HW trail ends at 16th St. & 1st Ave.

1.7 **LEFT** on 1st Ave., to 13th St.

RIGHT on 13th St., to 2nd Ave.

LEFT on 2nd Ave., a lovely pedestrian mall, through historic Navy Yard buildings, to intersection with Constitution Rd.

2.3 **LEFT** on Constitution Rd. and continue to intersection with Warren St., at Constitution Marina sign.

RIGHT on Warren St.

CROSS Chelsea St., continuing to Park St.

2.5 **RIGHT** on Park St., to delightful Winthrop common.

RIGHT on Common St., and run counterclockwise around the square, turning **LEFT** on Adams St. and **LEFT** on Winthrop St., returning to Warren St. Quintessential Charlestown!

2.8 **RIGHT** on Warren St., briefly to Monument Ave.

RIGHT on Monument Ave., up hill to Bunker Hill Monument at Monument Sq.

RUN UP to the Bunker Hill Monument, then around Monument Sq., ending up at Concord St.

3.3 **LEFT** on Concord St., briefly to Bartlett St.

RIGHT on Bartlett St., about ¼ mile to School St.

LEFT on School St., to High St.

RIGHT on High St. to the end, at Walker St.

3.7 **RIGHT** on Walker St., to Russell St.

LEFT on Russell St., to Mead St.

RIGHT on Mead St., going up the "seven stairs" to Bunker Hill St.

3.9 **RIGHT** on Bunker Hill St. After ¼ mile, Bunker Hill Cemetery on the left, nice water views. Continue to Green St.

4.2 **RIGHT** on Green St., following down hill to Main St.

4.5 **LEFT** on Main St. Historic Warren Tavern, interesting restaurants. Continue to major intersection.

BEAR RIGHT on Harvard St., through a lovely little square.

CONTINUE on Harvard St., through the John Harvard Mall, to the intersection with City Sq. and famous Olives Restaurant.

4.8 **RIGHT** at City Square, to the main road, Rt. 99/Rutherford Ave.

LEFT on Rutherford Ave., crossing over the Charlestown Bridge.

5.2 **RIGHT** on Causeway St., returning to North Station.

5.37 **END**

From the Water to Bunker Hill: Historic Charlestown

Mystic River

ENS John Doherty Playground

Terminal St

Mystic River Brg

Medford St

Baldwin St
Chappie St
Bunker Hill St
Auburn St
Oak St
Mead St
Russell St
Belmont St
Sackville St
Alston St
Mystic St
Wall St
Elm St
Polk St
Medford St

William J Barry Playground

5th Ave
16th St
3rd Ave
4th Ave
13th St
2nd Ave
1st Ave

Eden St
Walker St
Bartlett St
Pearl St
Concord Ave
Monument St
Oreilly Way
Walford Way
Bunker Hill St
Tufts St
Corey St
Obrien Ct
Medford St
Decatur St
Chelsea Ave

Sullivan St
Salem St
School St
Bartlett St
Bunker Hill Monument
Vine St
3rd Ave
7th St
9th St

High St
Green St
Cross St
Cedar St
Tremont St
Lowney Way
5th St
7th St
1st Ave

W School St
Cordis St
Pleasant St
Soley St
Mt Vernon St
Chestnut St
2nd Ave
Pier 7
8th St

Austin St
Warren St
Monument Av
Adams St
Baxter Rd

Union St
Main St
Winthrop St
Chelsea St
3rd Ave

Washington St
Harvard St
Park St
Lynde St
Henley St

New Rutherford Ave
City Sq
Chelsea St
Charlestown
Constitution Rd
USS Constitution

Bunker Hill Pavilion
Constitution Plz
Boston National Historic Park

US Coast Guard Station

North Point Park

Charlestown Brg
Paul Revere Pk
Langone Recreational Complex

Nashua Street Park
Nashua St
Martha Rd

Commercial St
Charter St
Hull St
Battery St
Old North Church

TD Banknorth Garden
Causeway St
MBTA North Station
Portland St
Friend St
Canal St
N Washington St
Lynn St
Endicott St
Prince St
Salem St
Tileston St
Hanover St
Clark St
Fleet St
Paul Revere House
North St

Blossom St
Merrimac St
Cooper St
Hillman St
Richmond St
Commercial St

Massachusetts General Hospital
New Chardon St
Cross St

N Grove St
Phillips St
Garden St
Irving St
Lloyd St
Buffinch Pl
Sudbury St
Cambridge St
Government Center At Scollay Square
Congress St
North St
Clinton St
Faneuil Hall
Holocaust Memorial Park
Atlantic Ave
Christopher Columbus Park

American NHS

99

1

93

3

LEGEND

Start/End

Route/Direction

1 Mile Marker

N North

Capitol Run

DISTANCE		
4.7 Miles	STARTING POINT	Kenmore Square
	TERRAIN	Flat; half of run is off-road
	LIGHTING	Well lit. Beautiful lights on trees on Comm. Ave. Mall
	BATHROOMS	Boston Common
	WATER	Boston Common, Public Garden
	INTERESTING SITES	State House, Boston Common, Public Garden, Commonwealth Ave. Mall, Charles river
	PARKING	Lots (expensive), meters
	PUBLIC TRANSPORTATION	T stations all over

Overview

This is one of the most historic and exciting city runs in the country, featuring some of Boston's most elegant and historic sites. In a little under 5 miles, runners can experience the brownstones of Back Bay, the Public Garden, Boston Common, the quaint shops along Charles St., and the Charles River path. All this is very jog-able. The loop begins with a jaunt along the Commonwealth Ave. Mall, the spine of the Back Bay, designed in the French Boulevard style in the 1850s. The run continues through the Public Garden, beautiful at any time of year, and then up Boston Common to the State House. The return is along the Boston side of the Charles River path. The route officially starts in Kenmore Square, but can be easily joined along any section and the mileage adjusted.

Distance Directions

START: Kenmore Square, Commonwealth Ave.

0.0 **EAST** on Commonwealth Ave. to Arlington St. Just east of Mass. Ave., use the Commonwealth Avenue Mall. Gracious old brownstones, specimen trees, and memorial statues, crossing the "H through A" streets from Hereford St. to Arlington St.

1.36 **CROSS** Arlington St., entering the Public Garden gate at the Washington statue and run through the Garden to traffic light. In season, the famous swan boats are on the right.

1.53 **CROSS** at the light (Charles St., no sign) into Boston Common.

LEFT on path in Common paralleling Charles St., to path at far north side of Common that runs alongside Beacon St.

RIGHT on path, to top of hill. State House is on the left.

2.0 **RETRACE STEPS DOWN HILL,** to the intersection of Beacon St. and Charles St.

Option: additional loop of Boston Common can add about 0.5m

2.38 **RIGHT** on Charles St., to the end, at Cambridge St. Charles St. is filled with lovely shops and restaurants and can be a little crowded for running.

2.73 **LEFT** at Cambridge St. (Charles Circle), at CVS. Go **OVER** the Charles/ MGH overpass, to where the path joins the river.

LEFT (WEST) on River Path, paralleling Storrow Drive, past the Longfellow Bridge, continuing to the Harvard Bridge at Massachusetts Ave.

Option: There are numerous options to do more along the river.

4.07 **UP** ramp at Harvard Bridge, and follow Mass. Ave. south, back to Commonwealth Ave.

4.27 **RIGHT** on Commonwealth Ave., returning to Kenmore Sq.

4.7 **END**

Back Bay Shopping Trip

ESSENTIALS		
DISTANCE **7.2** Miles *with many options for a longer or shorter route*	**STARTING POINT**	Boston Public Garden gate at Arlington St. and Commonwealth Ave.
	TERRAIN	Flat; sidewalks can be busy during business hours
	LIGHTING	Good
	BATHROOMS	In Back Bay T Station, on Boston Common
	WATER	Boston Common
	PUBLIC TRANSPORTATION	Numerous T stops in Back Bay.
	PARKING	Parking meters and public parking lots
	HIGHLIGHTS	Boston Common, State House, Public Garden, Commonwealth Ave. Mall, beautiful brownstones, Boston Public Library, Trinity Church, iconic Prudential Center and John Hancock Tower.

Overview

Most folks who run in Boston make a beeline for the River paths. This run covers the nicer streets of Back Bay, which features everything from beautiful brownstones, the European-esque Commonwealth Ave. Mall, the tony shops and galleries of Newbury St., and the wider Boylston St., with its many fine stores, restaurants, and architectural highlights at Copley Sq. The sidewalks are wide and the area is well lit at night. Newbury St. is very quiet and delightful for running before the stores open. This run offers numerous options for length. A good rule of thumb is that the main east-west running streets of Back Bay paralleling each other (Marlborough St., Newbury St., etc.) are 0.9 miles from Arlington St. to Mass Ave. This run is mainly confined to the Back Bay, keeping runners south of the river, north of Columbus Ave., and east of Massachusetts Ave.

An additional ½ mile or more can be added by looping around the perimeter of the Boston Common or by running on its numerous paths. Highlights of the Common are several inspiring statues, a skating rink in winter, playgrounds, and tennis courts. There is a wonderful farmer's market on Fridays in the late spring through fall right at Copley Sq, opposite the Boston Public Library.

START: Public Garden at Arlington St. and Commonwealth Ave. Mall

0.0   **WEST** along the Commonwealth Ave. Mall, about 1 mile, crossing Mass. Ave., to Charles Gate E.

1.1   **RIGHT** on Charles Gate E., to Beacon St.

      RIGHT on Beacon St. Continue along with views of the lovely brownstones to Arlington St.

2.3   **CROSS** Arlington St., into the Boston Common, and continue up the hill paralleling Beacon St. to the State House.

2.7   **RETURN DOWN PATH**, paralleling Beacon St., returning to Arlington St. and Beacon St.

3.2   **LEFT** on Arlington St., heading south, briefly to Marlborough St.

      RIGHT on Marlborough St., which is one of the more pleasant, quiet, and mainly residential streets of the Back Bay, to Mass. Ave.

4.2   **LEFT** on Mass. Ave., to Newbury St. Newbury St. features fine shops, restaurants, and galleries.

      LEFT on Newbury St., to Arlington St.

5.3   **RIGHT** on Arlington St., to Boylston St.

      RIGHT on Boylston St., to Mass. Ave. Boylston St. has wide sidewalks for running, as you enjoy the highlights at Copley Sq: Trinity Church, Boston Public Library, the John Hancock Tower, Prudential Center, and the newly opened luxurious Mandarin Oriental hotel.

6.2   **RIGHT** on Mass. Ave., back to Commonwealth Ave. Mall.

      RIGHT on Commonwealth Ave. Mall, back to Arlington St.

7.2   **END**

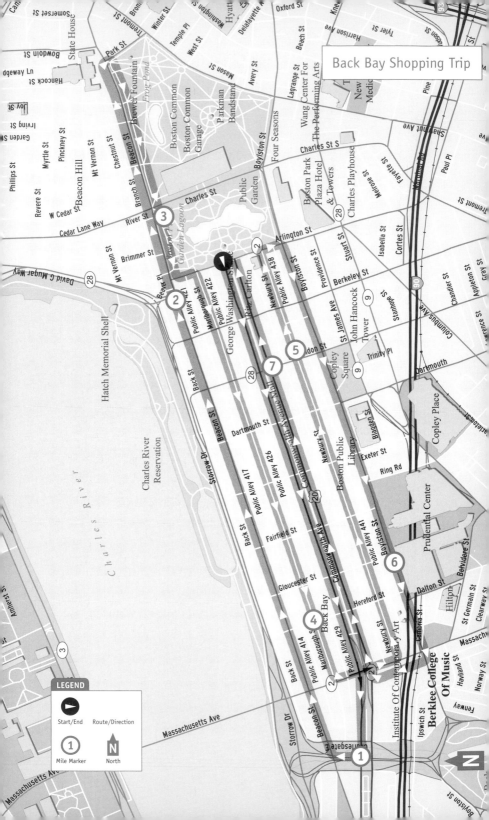

Back Bay Shopping Trip

LEGEND

Start/End   Route/Direction

1   N
Mile Marker   North

Gourmet Gallop:
Main Streets of the South End

ESSENTIALS		
DISTANCE 4.35 Miles	**STARTING POINT**	North Station
	TERRAIN	Flat; wide sidewalks on most streets
	LIGHTING	Good for running at night
	BATHROOMS	No public bathrooms
	WATER	In a couple of the parks
	PARKING	Limited meters & lots. Lots of "permit parking".
	PUBLIC TRANSPORTATION	Bounded by Back Bay and Mass. Ave.
	ADDITIONAL SPURS	SouthWest Corridor Park, p. 90; Side streets of South End, p. 34

Overview

The South End is a wonderful neighborhood for running in Boston. The main streets feature elegant buildings, restaurants, and an eclectic collection of shops. The side roads are lined with elegant Victorian-era residences and brownstones. Well-maintained squares and grassy medians calm traffic and give these side streets an Upper West Side feel.

This book features two distinct runs for the South End, although certain sections are interchangeable and could easily be combined. This "Gourmet Gallop" run highlights the main east-west thoroughfares of the South End. Tremont Street and Columbus Ave. feature a fine collection of interesting buildings, shops, and restaurants. Shawmut Ave. is often overlooked, having seen a fair bit of new development over the past several years. St. Botolph St. is more residential, and is a good connector to the Southwest Corridor Park. The section along Washington St. takes you by charming and historic Blackstone and Franklin Squares.

The main streets of the South End are very suitable for running, featuring good sidewalks and are quiet enough at certain times that running on the road is possible. It is also one of the better areas in Boston for runners because the main streets provide good "stretches" of about 0.8 miles between E. Berkeley St. and Mass. Ave.

Distance **Directions**

START: Public Garden at Arlington St. and Boylston St.

0.0　South on Arlington St., past the Park Plaza Hotel, to Columbus Ave.

0.12　**RIGHT** on Columbus Ave., which is one of the principal streets of the south end. Continue to the intersection with Massachusetts Ave.

1.0　**LEFT** on Mass. Ave., 0.1m to Tremont St.

1.1　**LEFT** on Tremont St., continuing 0.8m to E. Berkeley St. Tremont St. is one of the principal thoroughfares of the South End, linking the residential areas and featuring a great variety of shops and restaurants.

1.81　**RIGHT** on E. Berkeley St. to Shawmut Ave. Runners often overlook Shawmut Ave., but it has undergone many improvements in recent years.

1.96　**RIGHT** on Shawmut Ave., continuing back to Mass. Ave.

2.68　**LEFT** on Mass. Ave., briefly, to Washington St.

2.76　**LEFT** on Washington St., all the way to E. Berkeley St., taking in charming and historic Blackstone and Franklin Squares.

3.52　**LEFT** on E. Berkeley St. to Boylston St. Pass by Community Garden.

4.17　**RIGHT** on Boylston St., returning to the Public Garden.

4.35　**END**

Gourmet Gallop: Main Streets of the South End

LEGEND

⬤ Start/End

Route/Direction

① Mile Marker

N North

South End Softer Side:
Back Roads and Quiet Squares

ESSENTIALS		
DISTANCE **5.7** Miles	**STARTING POINT**	Public Garden, Arlington & Boylston St.
	TERRAIN	Flat; Some side streets are narrow
	LIGHTING	OK, but main roads are better
	BATHROOMS	No public bathrooms
	WATER	Peters Park
	INTERESTING SITES	Numerous small parks, squares, historic buildings
	PUBLIC TRANSPORTATION	Several options downtown
	PARKING	Limited meters & lots. "Permit Parking" galore
	ADDITIONAL SPURS	SouthWest Corridor Park, p. 90; Main streets of South End, p. 31

Overview

This run has quite a different character than the Main Streets of the South End. Here, you will enjoy the residential neighborhoods of the South End, which are very pleasant for running. These side streets, connecting to Tremont St. and Columbus Ave., feature elegant Victorian-era residences and brownstones, many of which have been renovated and restored in recent years. The streets have a distinct and unique neighborhood feel, with their well-maintained historic squares and tree-lined medians, punctuated by the occasional bakery or shop. Blackstone Square and Franklin Square, both laid out by Charles Bullfinch, adjoin one another and are the centerpieces of the south end, with their elegant design, fountains, and benches for resting. Concord Square, Rutland Square, and Union Park add a special character to their respective neighborhoods and help to calm traffic.

In designing this run, I have tried to keep you on the north-south streets that feature the longest stretches without a turn — though any run on the side streets of the South End will be more involved and complex than some of the other routes in this book. Use the specific route below as a guide: feel free to explore and vary, mix and match with the "Main Streets" run, and put together your own favorite South End jaunt.

START: Public Garden at Arlington St. and Boylston St.

Note: An alternative is to start right in the South End, at E. Berkeley and Appleton St., which saves about 0.6m of the run.

0.0 **SOUTH** on Arlington St. to intersection with Columbus Ave.

0.26 **RIGHT** on Columbus Ave., briefly to East Berkeley St.

0.40 **LEFT** on E. Berkeley St. to Appleton St. The Appleton Bakery is worth a post-run treat!

0.58 **RIGHT** on Appleton St., – a lovely, longer road – to end (W. Canton St.).

0.89 **LEFT** on W. Canton St., briefly to Warren Ave.

RIGHT on Warren Ave., which is similar in character to Appleton St., to the intersection with Columbus Ave. and W. Newton St.

LEFT on W. Newton St., crossing Tremont. This leads to two lovely squares. Blackstone Square was built in 1855 and Franklin Square in 1849.

1.39 **RUN THROUGH** Blackstone and Franklin Squares, to the intersection of St. George St. and East Newton St. *(Note: W. Newton St. turns into E. Newton St. at Shawmut Ave.)*

1.55 **WEST** on St. George St., to East Concord St.

RIGHT on E. Concord St., through lovely Concord Square to the intersection with Columbus Ave.

2.11 **RIGHT** on Columbus Ave., briefly, to Rutland St.

RIGHT on Rutland Square (restored in 2002), crossing Tremont St., to Shawmut Ave.

2.46 **LEFT** on Shawmut Ave., to Union Park St.

2.77 **LEFT** on Union Park St., through the quaint median of Union Park. The aptly named Buttery Bakery, is at Union Park and Shawmut St. At Tremont St. is a lovely square with the Cyclorama, new Calderwood Theater, and several terrific restaurants.

RIGHT on Tremont St. to Waltham St.

RIGHT on Waltham St. to Shawmut Ave.

3.08 **LEFT** on Shawmut Ave., continuing briefly to intersection with Dwight St. and Peters Park, which features a new playground and ballfield.

LEFT on Dwight St., returning to Tremont.

RIGHT on Tremont, to East Berkeley St.

LEFT on E. Berkeley St. Notice the community garden on the left.

3.42 **LEFT** on Warren St., 0.3m to the intersection with W. Canton St.

3.74 **RIGHT** on W. Canton St., crossing busy Columbus Ave., to St. Botolph St.

3.97 **LEFT** on St. Botolph St., which is delightfully residential, and continue 0.4m to the end (Mass. Ave.).

4.37 **LEFT** on Mass. Ave., very briefly, to the intersection with Southwest Corridor Park (Orange Line "T" Station is across the street).

LEFT on the Southwest Corridor Park pathway, and follow about ½ mile, to Dartmouth St. and the Back Bay "T" Station. A nice little detour, about halfway along the path between Mass. Ave. and Dartmouth St. is the small loop around Braddock Park.

4.95 **LEFT** on Dartmouth St., to the Commonwealth Ave. Mall.

5.29 **RIGHT** onto the Commonwealth Ave. Mall path until reaching the Public Garden at Arlington St.

5.67 **END**

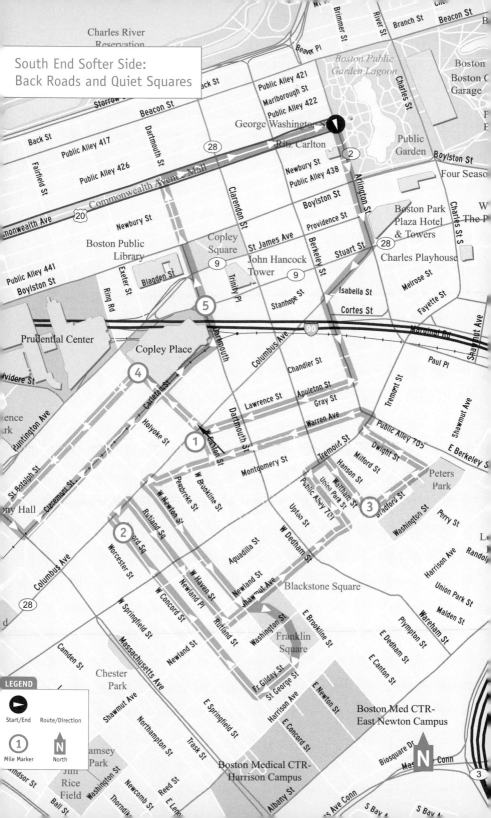

South End Softer Side:
Back Roads and Quiet Squares

Charles River
Reservation

Charles St

Brimmer St
River St
Branch St
Beacon St
Beaver Pl

Boston Public
Garden Lagoon

Boston
Boston C
Garage

Public Alley 421
Marlborough St
Public Alley 422

George Washington St

Ritz Carlton

Public
Garden

Storrow

Beacon St

Back St

Public Alley 417

Public Alley 426

Fairfield St

Dartmouth St

Commonwealth Avent Mall

Boylston St

Four Seas

(28)

(2)

Newbury St
Public Alley 438

Arlington St

Boston Park
Plaza Hotel
& Towers

The P

(20)

monwealth Ave

Newbury St

Clarendon St

Boylston St

Providence St

Charles St S

Boston Public
Library

Copley
Square

St James Ave

Berkeley St

Stuart St

(28)

Charles Playhouse

Public Alley 441

Exeter St

Blagden St

(9)

Trinity Pl

John Hancock
Tower

(9)

Melrose St

Fayette St

Boylston St

Ring Rd

Stanhope St

Prudential Center

(5)

Dartmouth St

Isabella St
Cortes St

Shawmut Ave

90

Columbus Ave

Paul Pl

Copley Place

Chandler St

Tremont St

videre St

(4)

Carleton St

Dartmouth St

Lawrence St
Apuleton St
Gray St
Warren Ave

Public Alley 705

Shawmut Ave

ence
k

Holyoke St

W Canton St

(1)

Montgomery St

Tremont St

Milford St

Dwight St

E Berkeley S

ny Hall

Claremont St

Pembroke St

W Brookline St

W Newton St

Rutland Sq

Hanson St
Waltham St
Public Alley 701
Union Park St

Bradford St

(3)

Peters
Park

Washington St

Perry St

(2)

ord Sq

Worcester St

Upton St

Washington St

L

Randol

(28)

Columbus Ave

W Springfield St

W Concord St

Aguadilla St

Newland St

W Dedham St

Blackstone Square

Harrison Ave

Union Park St

d

Camden St

Chester
Park

Massachusetts Ave

Shawmut Ave

Northampton St

W Haven St

Newland Pl

Rutland St

Shawmut Ave

Washington St

Franklin
Square

E Brookline St

E Dedham St

E Canton St

Plympton St

Wareham St

Malden St

Trask St

Fr Gilday St

St George St

E Newton St

Harrison Ave

E Concord St

E Springfield St

Boston Med CTR-
East Newton Campus

amsey
Park

Jim Rice
Field

Washington St

Reed St

Newcomb St

Albany St

Boston Medical CTR-
Harrison Campus

Biosquare Dr

Ma Conn

Mass Ave Conn

S Bay

S Bay

3

LEGEND

Start/End   Route/Direction

(1)
Mile Marker

N
North

Bakery Treat:
Arnold Arboretum to Roslindale Center

ESSENTIALS		
DISTANCE **4.5** Miles	**STARTING POINT**	Arnold Arboretum, Hunnewell Visitor Center
	TERRAIN	Gentle hills; much of run is off-road
	LIGHTING	Arboretum not lit or open at night
	BATHROOMS	Arboretum Visitor Center, commercial establishments in Roslindale
	WATER	Arboretum Visitor Center
	INTERESTING SITES	All the sights of Arnold Arboretum; restaurants and bakeries of Roslindale Square; spurs to Franklin Park, Forest Hills Cemetery
	PUBLIC TRANSPORTATION	Forest Hills T Station (Green & Orange Lines); Roslindale Square (Commuter Rail)
	PARKING	Available outside Arboretum
	ADDITIONAL SPURS	Franklin Park, Forest Hills Cemetery, Jamaica Pond

Overview

This is a great run to do on a Sunday morning, enjoying a mid-way treat at one of the many fine bakeries in Roslindale Square. The run starts at the Arnold Arboretum, featuring some of its most interesting paths (more detail on the Arboretum can be found on p. 117) to the Washington St. gate. You'll stay on South St., and then take Washington St. briefly to Roslindale Square. The Square has undergone many improvements over the past 15 years, and has been a centerpiece of Mayor Menino's Main Streets program. There are many fine, authentic bakeries and cafes in Roslindale. After enjoying your treat, the run loops back to the Arboretum along hilly Fairview St., which features an interesting mix of residential architecture. For variety, the return path through the Arboretum takes a different route back to the start.

It is possible to add several spurs to this run, particularly as you exit the Arboretum. There's the 2.2 mile loop around Franklin Park (p. 112), right across the way. Alternatively, Forest Hills Cemetery is a pleasure for runners with several miles of routes possible within its gates. For those desiring a longer, one-way run from the city out to Roslindale, one fun option is to use the Commuter Rail from Roslindale Square to return downtown (see the MBTA Web site for a specific schedule).

Distance **Directions**

START: Hunnewell Visitor Center @ Arborway Gate

0.0   **FOLLOW MEADOW RD.** from the Visitor Center, to end.

0.6   **RIGHT,** briefly, on Forest Hills Rd. Look for sign for Beech Path.

      TAKE Beech Path to intersection with South St.

0.8   **LEFT** at end of Beech Path, to South St. gate.

      RIGHT on South St. *(caution: no sign, narrow road).*

1.0   **STAY** on South St., at Bussey St., under underpass, crossing Archdale St., Lesher St., and Mosgrove St. in a more residential area.

1.6   **MERGE WITH** Washington St. **BEAR RIGHT** briefly, then **STAY ON SOUTH St.** where Washington St. branches off at a "green". South St. will take you into Roslindale Village.

      FOLLOW SOUTH ST. to Robert St. near the Commuter Rail Station. A nice detour into the Village features many fine shops, restaurants, and bakeries.

1.9   **RIGHT** on Robert St., at Alexander the Great Square, under train tracks, to intersection with S. Fairview St.

      RIGHT on S. Fairview St., which turns into Fairview St., up and down a hill. After ½ mile, see Arboretum's Mendum St. gate.

2.3   **ENTER** Arboretum.

      LEFT on Peter's Hill Rd., which loops around the perimeter of Peter's Hill. Run to the top of Peter's Hill., which at 235 feet, is the highest point in Boston.

2.7   **REJOIN** Peter's Hill Rd.

      RIGHT on Peter's Hill Rd. as you come down the hill.

2.9   **LEFT** at "T", briefly to Peter's Hill Gate.

      CROSS Bussey St. to the Bussey St. Gate.

      ENTER Bussey St. Gate, **BEARING SLIGHTLY RIGHT** on Hemlock Hill Rd. (no sign — you'll know you went the wrong way if you reach the Walter St. gate).

      FOLLOW Hemlock Hill Rd. to intersection (Valley Rd., no sign).

3.3   **LEFT** on Valley Rd. to another intersection.

3.6   **BEAR RIGHT** on Bussey Hill Rd. (no sign), clockwise along the perimeter of Bussey Hill, to intersection with Meadow Rd. and Forest Hills Rd.

4.0   **LEFT** onto Meadow Rd. in between the two ponds, and **FOLLOW** back to the Visitor Center.

      NOTE: An alternative, instead of rejoining Meadow Rd. is to take Linden Path, off Bussey Hill Rd., which can be seen on the Arboretum map.

4.5   **END**, at Visitor Center.

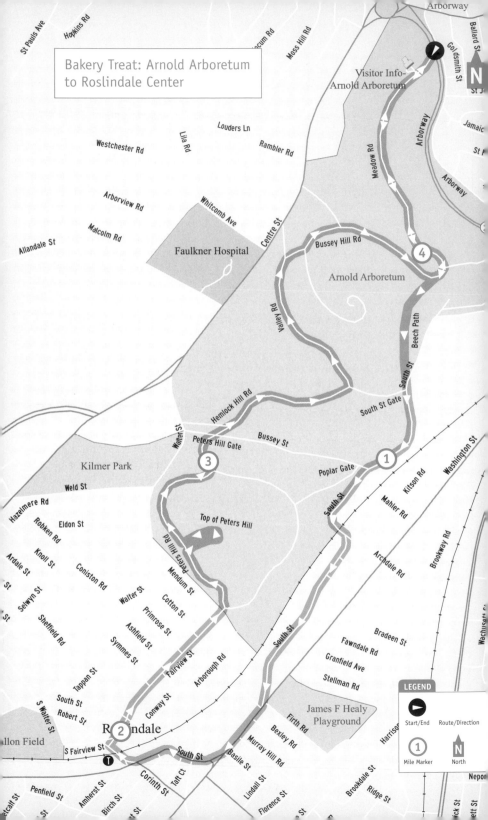

Bakery Treat: Arnold Arboretum
to Roslindale Center

Dip into Brookline

DISTANCE		
4.5 Miles	**STARTING POINT**	Kenmore Square
	TERRAIN	Flat; one-third of run is off-road
	LIGHTING	Streets well lit, except for last section on Riverway path.
	BATHROOMS	Commercial establishments along the way
	WATER	Amory Park, Longwood playground
	INTERESTING SITES	Pleasant residential neighborhoods; Historic Longwood Mall and Cottage Farm Historic District; Amory Park

Overview

Brookline is the closest-in western suburb of Boston. Within a half mile of Kenmore Square are some lovely residential neighborhoods with some spectacular, historic single family homes, built around attractive "squares" of quiet greens and specimen trees. The run features two particular neighborhoods, one on each side of Beacon Street. On the north side of Beacon, Amory St. leads into gracious Amory Park, which features clay tennis courts, a ball field, and a small path around Hall's pond. One of the highlights of this section is the Cottage Farm Historic District, featuring grand homes surrounding pretty Mason Square. Crossing over to the south side of Beacon, the highlight is Longwood Mall. The neighborhood has gone to great length to preserve some especially interesting and beautiful specimen trees. After enjoying some of the pleasant side roads near Brookline Village, the return is via the Riverway path, which is part of Olmsted Park.

Distance Directions

START: Kenmore Square

To reach Kenmore Square from Back Bay (Public Garden), add 1.3 miles along Commonwealth Ave.

0.0 **WEST** on Beacon St. for ½ mile, crossing over the Mass Pike., to St. Mary's Street. At St. Mary's, there's an old-fashioned breakfast place, the Busy Bee, a couple of bakeries, and a small grocery store called Fresh Market.

0.5 **RIGHT** on St. Mary's St., for one block, to Ivy St.

LEFT on Ivy St. This section features a tour of Mason Square.

RIGHT on Prescott St. to Euston St.

RIGHT on Euston St. to St. Mary's St.

LEFT on St. Mary's St.

LEFT on unmarked road through the square, back to Prescott.

RIGHT on Prescott St., briefly to Lenox St.

LEFT on Lenox St., one block, to Essex St.

LEFT on Essex St., one block, to Worthington St.

RIGHT on Worthington St. to Amory St. This section features the lovely Cottage Farm Historic District.

1.43 **LEFT** on Amory St., to entrance at Amory Park – a small driveway and parking lot.

1.58 **DO A SMALL LOOP** around Amory Park, ending up at other end, back onto Amory St.

LEFT on Amory St. to end, at Beacon St.

1.92 **RIGHT** on Beacon St., one block to Kent St.

CROSS Beacon St. and run two blocks to Chatham St., which is at the west end of the Longwood Mall. Note the beautiful specimen trees.

2.08 **LEFT** on Chatham St., to end (Hawes St., no sign).

RIGHT on Hawes St., to Beech Rd., to end at Kent St.

2.47 **LEFT** on Kent St., one block to Seawall Ave.

RIGHT on Seawall Ave. to Marshall St.

LEFT on Marshall St., to Longwood Ave. (no sign).

CROSS STREET at Longwood Ave., and proceed through the park (tennis courts, water fountain, Lawrence Elementary School). At the other end of the park is Francis St. and Toxteth St. *(Note: A nice detour is into Brookline Village, which features some interesting shops & restaurants.)*

2.79 **CROSS ONTO** Toxteth St., a pretty, village-y street. Continue to the end, at Aspinwall Ave.

LEFT on Aspinwall Ave. Cross Harrison St. and Kent St., following to Netherlands Rd.

3.14 **LEFT** on Netherlands Rd., to the entrance of the Riverway Path *(no sign, but path is evident)*.

LEFT on Riverway Path heading east, with "T" tracks on left and Riverway St. on right. Pass Longwood "T" Station on left. Continue on path to the end, at a small brick building at the intersection of Park Drive, and the Riverway/Fenway. The Fenway "T" station and Landmark Shopping Center (Staples, REI) are at the opposite end.

3.94 **LEFT** on Park Drive, which is busy road but has a decent sidewalk. Follow Park Drive to Beacon St.

4.11 **RIGHT** on Beacon St., returning to Kenmore Square.

4.56 **END**

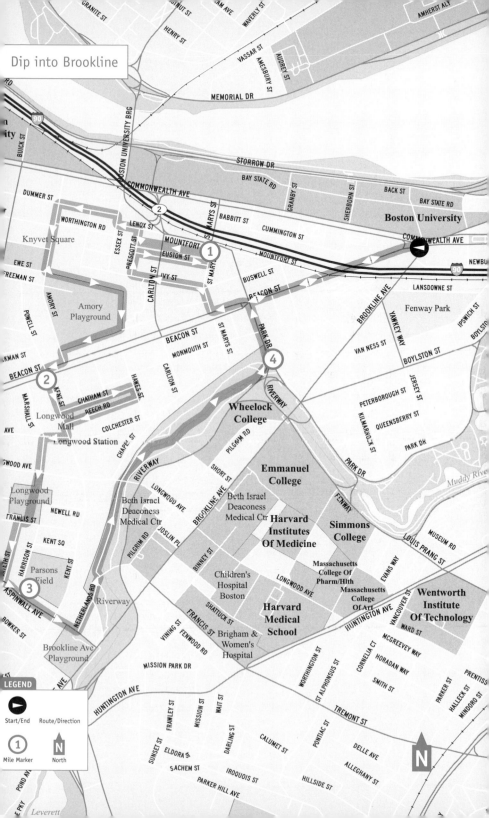

Dip into Brookline

GRANITE ST
CHESTNUT ST
HENRY ST
VASSAR ST
AMESBURY ST
AUDREY ST
WAVERLY ST
AM AVE
AMHERST ALY

MEMORIAL DR

DUMMER ST
WORTHINGTON RD
Knyvet Square
EWE ST
FREEMAN ST
AMORY ST
POWELL ST
LAKMAN ST
BEACON ST
MARSHALL ST
Longwood Mall
Longwood Station
AVE
NGWOOD AVE
Longwood Playground
FRANLIS ST
NEWELL RD
KENT SQ
HARRISON ST
Parsons Field
ASPINWALL AVE
BOWKER ST
Brookline Ave Playground
POND AVE
PKY
Leverett

STORROW DR
BAY STATE RD
COMMONWEALTH AVE
LENOX ST
MOUNTFORT
EUSTON ST
IVY ST
CARLTON ST
ESSEX ST
PRESCOTT ST
ST MARYS ST
BABBITT ST
GRANBY ST
CUMMINGTON ST
SHERBORN ST
BACK ST
BAY STATE RD

Boston University

COMMONWEALTH AVE
NEWBU
90

MOUNTFORT ST
BUSWELL ST
BEACON ST
LANSDOWNE ST

Amory Playground

BEACON ST
ST MARYS ST
MONMOUTH ST
CARLTON ST
PARK DR
Fenway Park
BROOKLINE AVE
YAWKEY WAY
VAN NESS ST
BOYLSTON ST
IPSWICH ST
BOYLSTO
JERSEY ST

RIVERWAY
Wheelock College
PETERBOROUGH ST
QUEENSBERRY ST
PARK DK

CHATHAM ST
KENT ST
BEECH RD
COLCHESTER ST
CHAPEL ST
RIVERWAY
PILGRIM RD
SHORT ST
LONGWOOD AVE
BROOKLINE AVE
Beth Israel Deaconess Medical Ctr
Beth Israel Deaconess Medical Ctr

Emmanuel College

Simmons College
FENWAY
PARK DR
Muddy River
LOUIS PRANG ST
MUSEUM RD

Harvard Institutes Of Medicine

Massachusetts College Of Pharm/Hlth
Massachusetts College Of Art

KENT ST
NETHERLANDS RD
PILGRIM RD
JOSLIN PL
BINNEY ST
Children's Hospital Boston
LONGWOOD AVE
Harvard Medical School
Brigham & Women's Hospital

Riverway

SHATTUCK ST
FRANCIS ST
VINING ST
FENWOOD RD
MISSION PARK DR
HUNTINGTON AVE
WORTHINGTON ST
ST ALPHONSUS ST
CORNELIA CT
HORADAN WAY
SMITH ST
MCGREEVEY WAY
WARD ST
EVANS WAY
VANCOUVER ST
HUNTINGTON AVE

Wentworth Institute Of Technology

PARKER ST
HALLECK ST
MINDORO ST
PRENTISS

SUNSET ST
ELDORA ST
FRAWLEY ST
MISSION ST
WAIT ST
DARLING ST
CALUMET ST
SACHEM ST
IROQUOIS ST
PARKER HILL AVE
PONTIAC ST
TREMONT ST
DELLE AVE
ALLEGHANY ST
HILLSIDE AVE

N

LEGEND

Start/End   Route/Direction

1
Mile Marker   North

Three Pond Tour: Jamaica Pond, Brookline Reservoir, Chestnut Hill Reservoir

ESSENTIALS		
DISTANCE **12.1** Miles	**STARTING POINT**	Kenmore Square
	TERRAIN	Some hills in Fisher Hill neighborhood; paths around ponds are dirt.
	LIGHTING	Ponds and paths not well lit at night
	BATHROOMS	Jamaica Pond boat house; commercial establishments along Beacon St.
	WATER	Public fountain at Jamaica Pond boat house
	INTERESTING SITES	Jamaica Pond, Brookline Reservoir, Chestnut Hill Reservoir, Emerald Necklace Riverway Paths, Estates of Fisher Hill area
	PUBLIC TRANSPORTATION	Green line at Kenmore Sq. Fenway, and C-line along Beacon St.

Overview

This is one of the longer runs in the book, at just over 12 miles, and it is also very rewarding. The centerpiece is a tour of three ponds/reservoirs near Boston, each of them having a dedicated, off-road path around their perimeter. The connections between the ponds are delightful, and include the Riverway paths of Olmsted Park and the beautiful roads and homes of the Fisher Hill neighborhood. One option to shorten the run is to take the Green Line back into the city from Cleveland Circle, saving the final three miles along Beacon St.

The run starts in Kenmore Square, soon joining the Riverway path through Olmsted Park to Jamaica Pond. After the 1.45 mile loop around Jamaica Pond, you will connect to the Brookline Reservoir, which straddles Rt. 9. The path around is just short of a mile and features lovely views of the city. The connection to the 1.5 mile loop around the Chestnut Hill Reservoir is through the pleasant roads and beautiful homes of Brookline's Fisher Hill neighborhood. The return to Boston is straight along Beacon St., which is quite pleasant for running, featuring wide sidewalks, a bike lane in sections, good lighting, and the interesting commercial areas of Washington Square and Coolidge Corner.

Distance	Directions

START: Kenmore Square

0.0   **WEST** along Beacon St. for about ½ mile, crossing over the Pike. Good views of Fenway Park.

0.4   **LEFT** on Park Rd., staying on the west side.

        RIGHT at small brick building, across from Fenway T station and Landmark shopping center (Staples, REI), onto Riverway path. See "bike route" sign.

        FOLLOW the Riverway Path, past Longwood T station on right to the complex intersection of Rt. 9, Riverway/Jamaicaway. *NOTE: Tricky crossings at Netherlands Rd. and Brookline Ave., keep eye out for path (no signs). The path ends abruptly, and temporarily, at River St.*

1.6   **TAKE** River St., leaving Riverway Path briefly (Brookline Ice Co. on right).

        CROSS Rt. 9 at busy intersection at the end of River St. Continuation of the Riverway path is at Olmsted Park sign, with Pond St. on right.

1.7   **FOLLOW** the Riverway Path through Olmsted Park, with Leverett Pond on the left. Delightful section for running, separate paths for walkers and bikers. Continue along the path, to a traffic light at Perkins St.

2.5   **CROSS** Perkins St., and run the 1.45m loop around Jamaica Pond, passing the historic boathouse (water, restrooms) ¾ of the way around.

4.0   **EXIT** the pond path and run along Perkins St., paralleling the pond path.

        FOLLOW Perkins St. for about ½ mile, crossing Parkman Dr. and Prince St., to Cottage St.

4.5   **RIGHT** on Cottage St., to end, and intersection with Warren St.

4.7   **RIGHT** on Warren St., following for about ½ mile *(Caution: Warren St. is narrow in parts).* After crossing Walnut St. and just short of Rt. 9, see entrance to the Brookline Reservoir on the left.

5.2   **ENTER** the Brookline Reservoir and run the 0.9m loop around the stone dust path. **RETURN** to path entrance at Warren St.

6.1   **CROSS** Rt. 9 at Warren St. and traffic light. This becomes Sumner Rd.

        STRAIGHT on Sumner Rd., to Buckminster Rd.

6.3   **LEFT** on Buckminster Rd. This is a quiet street featuring impressive homes. Follow Buckminster Rd. to the intersection with Fisher Ave.

6.9   **RIGHT** on Fisher Ave., down the hill, crossing Dean Rd., to Clinton Rd.

7.1   **LEFT** on Clinton Rd., briefly to Chestnut Hill Ave. *(Caution: busy area, challenging crossing.)*

        RIGHT on Chestnut Hill Ave., past Reservoir T station (D-Line).

7.3   **LEFT** on Beacon St., at Cleveland Circle, heading West.

Continued on page 48

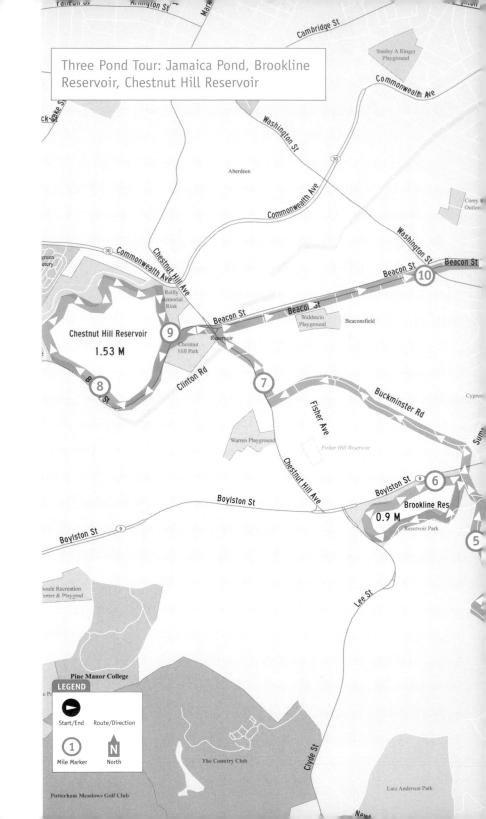

Three Pond Tour: Jamaica Pond, Brookline
Reservoir, Chestnut Hill Reservoir

Chestnut Hill Reservoir
1.53 M

Brookline Res
0.9 M

LEGEND

Start/End   Route/Direction

1   N

Mile Marker   North

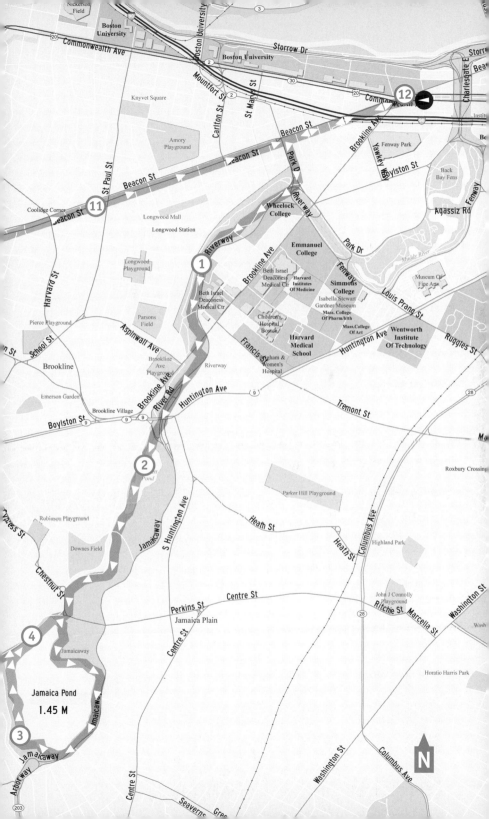

Just ahead, past Cassidy Playground and the Daly Rink, enter the Chestnut Hill Reservoir, going up the main stairs.

7.5 **ENTER** Chestnut Hill Reservoir, and enjoy the 1.5 mile loop around on a recently improved stone dust path, with great water views, BC to the west and the city skyline to the east.

9.0 **EXIT** Reservoir path after completing the loop.

TAKE Beacon St., heading **EAST**. *(NOTE: If you want to end the run here, it is possible to return to Boston via the C-Line, which runs along Beacon St.)*

9.2 **EAST** on Beacon St. at Cleveland Circle, for 2.9 m, returning to Kenmore Sq. Beacon St. becomes pleasant for running as it heads into Brookline, featuring wide sidewalks and good lighting.

10.0 Washington Square (restaurants, Starbucks), at Washington St.

10.8 Coolidge Corner at Harvard St. (stores, restaurants, Coolidge Corner Theater, Brookline Booksmith)

11.6 Park Drive

12.1 **END**

Beacon Street Special

ESSENTIALS		
DISTANCE Up to # 10 miles, with many options for segments	**STARTING POINT**	Any point on Beacon St.
	TERRAIN	Moderately hilly in spots. Hilliest through Chestnut Hill section in Newton.
	LIGHTING	One of the best places to run at night. Widest sidewalks and best lit sections are between the city and Cleveland Circle.
	BATHROOMS	Starbucks in Coolidge Corner, Washington Square, Newton Center, Waban
	WATER	Commercial spots along the way. Cold Spring Park in Newton.
	INTERESTING SITES	BC Campus, Chestnut Hill Reservoir, Mary Baker Eddy Home
	PUBLIC TRANSPORTATION	Green Line C line runs along Beacon St. from Kenmore Sq. to Cleveland Circle. D Line stops at Newton Center, Waban Center, Woodland.
	PARKING	Meters along Beacon St., free on side roads
	ADD-ON SPURS	Numerous neighborhoods and side roads off Beacon St. Chestnut Hill Reservoir is 1.5 miles around; nice paths in Cold Spring Park in Newton.

Overview

A run along Beacon St. is iconic in exposing Boston's character as it starts at the State House on Boston Common and then heads out to the suburbs of Brookline and Newton, to its end 10 miles later at Rt. 16/Washington St. Starting at Boston Common, the first part of the run features the beautiful brownstones of Back Bay. Kenmore Square is the transition point, as Beacon heads into Brookline, and then Newton, becoming leafier and greener as it heads west, passing through commercial areas and village centers every mile or so. At Cleveland Circle, which borders Brookline and Newton, you will run along the lovely Chestnut Hill Reservoir for 0.7 miles.

The run along Beacon Street is surprisingly pleasant. There are cars, but most of Beacon St. is pleasantly shaded, featuring wide sidewalks and good lighting. Beacon Street in Brookline has undergone recent improvements: period lighting, new trees, and a bike lane in sections. In parts of Newton, in addition to good sidewalks, it is possible to run on the road in the extra lane that is sort of a bike path but not marked as such. Beacon St. is also good for running in winter because, as a main road, it is one of the first to be cleared of snow.

This run is entirely along Beacon St., with major cross streets and distances given between the State House on Boston Common and Rt. 16/Washington St. in Newton. There is no set distance for this run. Runners can start along any section and do as much as they like. The total distance from Boston Common to Rt. 16/Washington St. in Newton is almost exactly 10 miles. One fun option is to run one-way out, and then hop the T back. The C-line runs along Beacon St. from Kenmore Square to Cleveland Circle. There are D-Line stops along the route in Newton Center, Waban Center, and then Woodland, which is 0.3 miles east of the intersection of Beacon St. and Rt. 16/Washington St. in Newton. T-Stops along the route are indicated.

Beacon Street Segment Distances

Section	Segment Distance	Total Distance	T Stop
State House to Kenmore Square	1.80	1.80	B-E line
Kenmore Square to Coolidge Corner	1.33	3.13	C-line
Coolidge Corner to Washington Sq.	0.75	3.88	C-line
Washington Square to Cleveland Circle	0.80	4.68	C-line
Cleveland Circle to Hammond Pond Pkwy.	1.78	6.46	
Hammond Pond Pkwy to Newton Center	0.72	7.18	D-line
Newton Center to Walnut St.	0.64	7.82	
Walnut St. to Waban Center	1.31	9.13	D-line
Waban Center to Rt. 16/Washington St.	0.94	10.1	D-line
(Woodland T Station is on Rt. 16, 0.3m east of the Beacon St./Rt. 16 intersection)			

Marathon Trainer

ESSENTIALS		
DISTANCE **11.6** miles; option for "Half-Marathon"	**STARTING POINT**	Cleveland Circle, bordering Brookline and Newton. Carriage road starts at Boston College T station.
	TERRAIN	Moderately hilly. Dirt/grass path along median of Comm. Ave.
	LIGHTING	OK for running in the dark
	BATHROOMS	Newton Public Library
	WATER	Newton Public Library
	INTERESTING SITES	Chestnut Hill Reservoir, lovely homes along Commonwealth Ave., Marathon markers, Newton City Hall, Brae Burn Country Club.

Overview

This run combines the Beacon St. and Commonwealth Ave. runs to create a long loop, following much of the inner ten miles of the Boston Marathon Route. Starting in Cleveland Circle, the route west features the Commonwealth Ave. carriage road, which is a magnet for runners, with little traffic, lovely homes, and rolling hills. You'll then loop over to Beacon St. on Rt. 16 in Newton, returning via Beacon St. through Waban Center and Newton Center. Even though both Commonwealth Ave. and Beacon St. are busy main roads, they are pleasant for running. The full run is 11.6 miles, but can be made into a half-marathon by running one loop around Chestnut Hill Reservoir at the beginning or end of the tour. The run can also be extended by 2.9 miles one way from Kenmore Square to Cleveland Circle.

Distance Directions

START: Cleveland Circle

0.0   **WEST** on Beacon St. from Cleveland Circle, briefly to entrance to Chestnut Hill Reservoir. Run half way around the Reservoir, 0.8 m to Chestnut Hill Drwy./Sir Thomas Moore Rd.

0.8   **RIGHT** on Chestnut Hill Drwy. At fork, **STAY LEFT** on Sir Thomas Moore Rd. Head to traffic light (Commonwealth Ave./Rt. 30).

1.37   **LEFT** on Commonwealth Ave., heading west. The carriage road begins right after the cluster of retail stores at the Boston College T station (B line). Run along Commonwealth Ave., passing Hammond St., Center St., Walnut St., and Chestnut St., to Rt. 16/Washington St.

5.28   **LEFT** on Rt. 16/Washington St. Head west nearly 1 mile, to Beacon St., which is just past Newton-Wellesley Hospital at a traffic light.

6.20 **LEFT** on Beacon St, heading east. Follow Beacon St. 5.4 miles through Waban Center and Newton Center, to Cleveland Circle.

11.59 **END**

To make this a Half-Marathon: At Cleveland Circle, run the 1.5 mile loop around the Chestnut Hill Reservoir, bringing the total to 13.1 miles.

Add-on Spurs:

- Starting in Kenmore Square, using Beacon St. to Cleveland Circle, adds 2.88 miles each way, for 5.76 miles
- Circuit around Chestnut Hill Reservoir: 1.5 miles

Segment Distances

Section	Segment Distance	Total Distance
Commonwealth Ave. Section, Heading West		
Cleveland Circle to Comm. Ave. Carriage Rd.	1.37	1.37
Carriage Rd. to Hammond St.	0.63	2.00
Hammond St. to Center St.	0.76	2.76
Newton Center to Walnut St.	0.76	3.52
Walnut St. to Chestnut St.	0.90	4.42
Chestnut St. to Rt. 16/Washington St.	0.86	5.28
Rt. 16/Washington St. to Beacon St.	0.92	6.20
Beacon St., Heading East		
Rt. 16 to Waban Center	0.94	7.14
Waban Center to Walnut St.	1.31	8.45
Walnut St. to Newton Center	0.64	9.09
Newton Center to Hammond Pond Pkwy.	0.72	9.81
Hammond Pond Pkwy. to Cleveland Circle	1.78	11.59
Add-On from Cleveland Circle to Kenmore Square, along Beacon St.		
Cleveland Circle to Washington Square	0.80	12.39
Washington Square to Coolidge Corner	0.75	13.14
Coolidge Corner to Kenmore Square	1.33	14.47

Running Boston's HarborWalk: An Overview

Overview

The continually improving and expanding HarborWalk trail has become one of Boston's running highlights. There are some absolutely spectacular sections of the HarborWalk for running in and near downtown Boston. Numerous organizations and individuals have worked hard to improve public access, install signage, and design parks and other ways of enjoying one of Boston's great assets. Nearly 38 out of a planned 47 miles have been completed, and every year, new "access points" are being opened, each of them with different character and features. The HarborWalk *officially* begins in East Boston, but the "seamless" path stretches from Charlestown to Quincy, with the occasional interruption.

It should be noted that the HarborWalk is a combination of off-road "trail", access/observation points, and sections along main roads on or near the water. And because the HarborWalk goes around marinas, up and down piers, and on some privately owned land, it is not a seamless linear path. Note also that in a couple of sections, particularly around Fort Point Channel and the Seaport district, there are options for spurs that go off the main HarborWalk trail. Nearly all of the HarborWalk features fine water views. About three-quarters of the route is on a dedicated "path", with HarborWalk signs along much of the way. There are a few sections where the HarborWalk is interrupted — due to inexplicably closed gates or incomplete sections — and there is the occasional missing or confusing sign. My recommendation is to follow the directions below very carefully once, and then you will know the idiosyncrasies of the route. But also bear in mind that the HarborWalk is continually evolving, so there might be changes even by the time this book is published!

This book provides many options for enjoying the HarborWalk, whether out for a casual jog, long run, or pleasant walk:

- **Several "loop" or "there and back" runs,** for sections of the HarborWalk
  - North Station to Fort Point Channel and Back, p.63
  - Charlestown Spur p. 66; Fort Point Channel Spur, p. 69
- **The HarborWalk One-Way,** from Charlestown to UMASS Boston at Rt. 3A, divided into three sections:
  - HarborWalk sections in detail, p. 56-62
  - Table detailing the section segment lengths, p. 55

- **Select HarborWalk sections,** not connected by foot to the main Charlestown-UMASS HarborWalk, notably in East Boston and south of UMASS, connecting to the Neponset River Greenway.
  - East Boston sections, featuring Piers Point, Hyatt Harborside, Constitution Beach, Bell Isle Marsh, p. 79
  - Deer Island and Winthrop Shore Drive, p. 76

My favorite sections of the downtown HarborWalk are around the USS Constitution in Charlestown, and then starting again at the Boston Aquarium, to Fort Point Channel, featuring the Boston Harbor Hotel, Northern Avenue Bridge, the Moakley Courthouse, the new Institute of Contemporary Art, and Fan Pier. Another spectacular section of the HarborWalk is the nearly 6-mile section starting in South Boston at Pleasure Bay and continuing to UMASS Boston at the intersection with Morrissey Blvd. The 1.6 mile connection between the downtown and South Boston sections of the HarborWalk, mainly using Summer St., is a little more industrial but is well-marked and suitable for running. East Boston, while not connected to the rest of the HarborWalk by foot, features some wonderful running options. The 2.6 mile loop around Deer Island is unique, with spectacular water and skyline views encircling the Taj Mahal of waste treatment plants. The newly developed sections close to the airport, notably Piers Park and Harborside Drive, going by the Hyatt Hotel, offer dynamite views of the water and Boston skyline.

There are several resources for more detail on the HarborWalk. See **www.bostonharborwalk.com** for an interactive map of the entire HarborWalk.

The Entire HarborWalk In Sections

The table below is for those who want to do enjoy particular sections of the HarborWalk, one way. The total, from 16th St. in Charlestown to UMASS Boston, is 12.7 miles. Also included in the table are major T stations, allowing runners to return to North Station or other points downtown.

The official northern point of the HarborWalk section in this book starts in Charlestown, at 16th St. and 1st Ave. It terminates at the UMASS Boston Campus at Rt. 3A/Morrissey Blvd., overlooking Dorchester Bay. From there, a 1.6 mile connection can be made to the approximately 3-mile Neponset River Greenway. And across the water in East Boston and Winthrop, there are several miles of lovely waterfront paths, though one must drive or take the T to access East Boston from downtown.

See chart on next page.

HarborWalk Sections

Section	Segment Distance	Total Distance	Restrooms/ Water	T to Return
Charlestown 16th St. & 1st Ave to North Station @ Beverly St. extension	1.5	1.5	USS. Const. Museum	
N. Station @ 131 Beverly St. Ext. to Aquarium	1.4	2.9	Aquarium	Aquarium Blue Line
Aquarium to Seaport World Trade Center @ Commonwealth Pier	1.3	4.2		World Trade Ctr. Silver Line
Around Commonwealth Pier to Pleasure Bay (Head Island Causeway & Day Blvd. intersection) via Summer St.	2.6	6.8	Head Island Playground	
Around Pleasure Bay & Castle Island, to William Day Blvd.	2.1	8.9	Head Island playground	
William Day Blvd. to McCormack Bath House @ Carson Beach	1.6	10.5	McCormack Bath House	
Carson Beach to JFK Library (front dock)	1.3	11.8	JFK Library	
JFK Library to UMASS Boston @ Rt. 3A Intersection	0.9	12.7		JFK/UMASS Red Line/ Commuter Rail
Connection to Neponset River Greenway start at Tenean Beach	1.6	14.3	Tenean Beach	
Neponset River Greenway (Tenean Beach to Central Ave. T Station)	3.0	17.3	Pope John Paul II Park	Central Ave. Red Line

Note: distances are approximate.

55

HarborWalk One-Way, Section 1:
Charlestown to Aquarium
2.9 Miles

Note: See p. 63 for a detailed description of the features of this section.

Distance Directions

START: Charlestown, @16th St. and 1st Ave.

0.0   At 16th St. and 1st Ave., follow HW signs past Piers 8, 7, 6, and 5 along the water to the USS Constitution Museum.

0.5   Follow Constitution Rd., out gate to Paul Revere Park, just past the Constitution Landing Sign and the Marriott Residence Inn.

      ENTER park, and **CROSS** floating sidewalk where the New Charles River Basin sign is on the brick building, to the Police Marine Division parking lot at Lovejoy Wharf.

1.4   **PROCEED BRIEFLY** to the parking lot on the left. Small ramp, **NO SIGN**, @ 131 Beverly St. building.

      GET ONTO RAMP at 131 Beverly St. sign, which goes underneath the Charlestown Bridge toward the North End. Terrific view of the Zakim Bridge.

      CONTINUE ON PATH along the water, to Commercial St. at the Mirabella Pool.

2.0   **SOUTH** (toward downtown) on Commercial St. *(NOTE: very soon there is another HarborWalk sign, but presently there is a locked gate.)* Cross Hanover St., to Battery Wharf.

      LEFT on Battery St., following HW sign for Burroughs Wharf. Lovely views.

      FOLLOW HW around, exiting at Union Wharf parking lot back to Commercial St.

2.3   **LEFT**, proceeding **SOUTH** on Commercial St. *(Note: Commercial St. turns into Atlantic Ave.)*

      LEFT at Sargent's Wharf, picking up HW sign again, to Lewis Wharf.

      EXIT Lewis Wharf to Atlantic Ave.

2.6   **LEFT** on Atlantic Ave., proceeding south. Here the relatively seamless HarborWalk along the water begins. Pass Joe's restaurant, to the intersection of Long Wharf, Christopher Columbus Park, and the Marriott hotel. This is a festive area, always filled with people.

      FOLLOW HW trail, around Long Wharf, to the Aquarium.

2.9   **END SECTION 1**

HarborWalk One-Way, Section 1:
Charlestown to Aquarium

Medford St
Walford Way
Oreilly Way
16th St
5th Ave
5th St
Corey St
Obrien Ct
4th Ave
3rd Ave
Decatur St
Chelsea St
2nd Ave
13th St
3rd Ave
9th St
1st Ave
Pier 7
7th St
6th St
8th St
Lowney Way
5th St
6th St
2nd Ave
Baxter Rd
3rd St
USS Constitution
Bunker Hill Pavilion
Boston National
Historic Park
Charlestown
Chelsea St
Constitution Rd
Constitution Plz
Harvard St
Henley St
City Sq
Main St
Chestnut St
Mt Vernon St
Cordis St
Pleasant St
Monument Ave
Soley St
Winthrop St
Adams St
Park St
Tremont St
Pearl St
Paul Revere Pk
Charlestown Brg
(Boardwalk under bridge)
Langone
Recreational Complex
US Coast Guard
Station
Commercial St
Causeway St
MBTA North
Station
N Washington St
Charter St
Hull St
Salem St
Tileston St
Old North Church
Battery St
Callahan
Canal St
Friend St
Portland St
Lynn St
Endicott St
Prince St
Clark St
Union Wharf
Merrimac St
Cooper St
Hanover St
Fleet St
Paul Revere House
Lewis Wharf
New Chardon St
Stillman St
North St
Richmond St
Commercial St
Commercial Wharf
Bulfinch Pl
Cross St
Commercial Ave
Christopher
Columbus Park
North
Garden
Holocaust
Memorial
Park
Atlantic Ave
New England Aq
LEGEND
Government
Center At
Scollay
Square
Congress St
Clinton St
Faneuil Hall
Marketplace
Long Whrf
Start/End
Route/Direction
Sudbury St
North St
Court St
State St
Chatham St
Boston City Hall
Kilby St
Broad St
Milk St
Boston
Old City Hall
School St
Water St
John F Fitzgerald Surface
N
Mile Marker
North
99
1
1
93
2
1
1
3
2.9

HarborWalk One-Way, Section 2:
Aquarium to Pleasure Bay, South Boston
3.9 Miles

Distance	Directions

START: Aquarium T Station

2.9   **CONTINUE** on the HW trail from Aquarium to Rowes Wharf.

CONTINUE past Rowes Wharf along the HW, behind the Boston Harbor Hotel and the spectacular domed walkway with a view to downtown. Just after hotel, is the Northern Ave. pedestrian bridge and the famous James Hook Lobster Co.

3.5   **LEFT** onto pedestrian bridge.

PROCEED ALONG WATER after the bridge, following the HW around the outside of the Federal Courthouse building, then along the wonderful Fan Pier section, to the new Institute of Contemporary Art.

GO AROUND the outside of the ICA, staying on the water, to Putnam Plaza, at Anthony's Pier 4 restaurant. Come out onto Seaport Blvd.

LEFT on Seaport Blvd, briefly, to the sign that says Seaport World Trade Center.

4.2   **LEFT** at the Seaport World Trade Center sign (Dunkin' Donuts), following Commonwealth Pier around, with nice water views. Come back out to Seapoint Blvd./Northern Ave.

4.84   At Commonwealth Pier and Northern Ave., **GO UP ESCALATOR** inside the World Trade Center building to the elevated World Trade Center Ave., toward the Convention Center (if you miss this, take D Street south).

5.07   **LEFT** on Summer St. This section is a bit industrial, but OK for running.

CROSS D St., E St., Pappas Way/Drydock Ave., to intersection with E. 2nd St.

5.94   **LEFT** on E. 2nd St. Pass by Christopher Lee Playground, Independence Sq., **JOGGING SLIGHTLY RIGHT AT M ST. TO CONTINUE** on 2nd St., to end (Farragut Rd.).

6.47   **RIGHT** on Farragut Rd., to intersection with E. Broadway. Notice Farragut Statue, in honor of one of Boston's leading Civil War generals.

LEFT on E. Broadway, then 1 block to William J Day Blvd in Marine Park.

RIGHT on Marine Blvd. to intersection with Head Island Causeway.

6.8   **END SECTION 2**

HarborWalk One-Way, Section 2: Aquarium to Pleasure Bay

Jeffries Point

Joe Porzio Park

Christopher Columbus Park

New England Aquarium

2.9

Rowes Wharf

Moakley Courthouse

N. Ave. Ped Bridge

Boston Tea Party Ship And Museum

ICA

4

Commonwealth Pier

Seaport Blvd

Children's Museum Of Boston

Summer St

Seaport World Trade Center

W Service Rd Ext

Congress St

B St

WTC Ave

Northern Ave

5

Summer St

Boston Convention & Exhibition Ctr

D St

Economic Dev Industrial Corporation

W 1st St

E 1st St

Reserved Channel

Summer St

Christopher Lee Play

Marine Park

6

E 2nd St

Independence Square Park

City Point

Pleasure Bay Park

W Broadway

E Broadway

Farragut Rd

Day Blvd

6.8

Dorchester Hts Nat'l Site

L St

Dorchester Heights

William J Day Blvd

L St Beach

For

John F Fitzgerald Surface Rd

Atlantic

Church

1

LEGEND

Start/End   Route/Direction

1   N

Mile Marker   North

HarborWalk One-Way, Section 3:
Pleasure Bay to UMASS Boston
5.9 Miles

Distance	Directions
START	Intersection of Day Blvd. and Head Island Causeway
6.8	**LEFT** at Pleasure Bay sign onto Head Island Causeway
	COUNTERCLOCKWISE AROUND PERIMETER of Pleasure Bay, Head Island, & Fort Independence Park. On Castle Island there is a playground, a beach, and a snack bar. Return to the intersection of William Day Blvd. and Head Island Causeway.
8.9	**SOUTH** along William Day Blvd., passing City Beach, the L Street Bath House, and several Yacht Clubs.
	LEAVE DAY BLVD. onto the waterfront path, opposite Moakley Park.
	Continue for 1.5 miles to Carson Beach. The McCormack Bath House features a snack bar, public restrooms (seasonal).
10.5	**CONTINUE** past Carson Beach, following main pathway along water. The JFK Library is ahead. Lovely section here.
	NOTE: The path does not continue exactly to the JFK Library. Just before the library, proceed right, off the path and up a hill. Go over the hill, and continue down to the Library and re-enter the path. Continue around, to the other side of the Library and dock with great views of Dorchester Bay.
11.8	**CONTINUE** south from the JFK Library, along the HW path south to UMASS Boston. There are great views out to Dorchester Bay on the left, with the UMASS campus and state Archives building on the right. Stay on the path until the intersection with Rt. 3A/Morrissey Blvd.
12.7	**END SECTION 3**

See page 61 for connection to Neponset River Greenway.

Additional Spur: Connection to Neponset River Greenway

If you want to add even more, it is a (not very pleasant) 1.6 miles from UMASS Boston to the northern terminus of the (very pleasant) 3-mile Neponset River Greenway. You can run to the south end of the Greenway at the Central Ave. Red Line station and take the "T" back. See p. 126 for the entire Neponset River Greenway run.

Distance **Directions**

12.7 **LEFT** on Rt. 3A/Morrissey Blvd. This section is busy, but there is a sidewalk. Notice the Vietnam Veterans Memorial on the left. Continue to intersection with Freeport St.

Detour Option: Malibu Beach/Savin Hill Park, on the right, is a recently upgraded area with a pleasant walking path around the water (about 1/2m around the perimeter), a playground, picnic benches, a protected beach, drinking water, and restrooms.

13.6 **BEAR SLIGHTLY LEFT** on Freeport St. (Toyota dealership, HW sign). Continue along Freeport St. Parts of this have no path or sidewalk.

Detour Option: Victory Rd. leads to Victory Park, a pleasant 0.3 m dirt path along the water. This is part of the HarborWalk, but unfortunately it does not connect to the next section, Tenean Beach.

STAY on Freeport St. See signs for the Neponset River Greenway (NRG) path. Stop for a treat at a great, old-fashioned candy store, Phillips Candy House, which has been there since 1925! Freeport St. turns into Tenean St. just after the Candy House. Follow the HW and NRG signs to Tenean Beach.

14.3 **END**

Note: At this point, the HW does continue for a bit, but we end the official HW "run" here. Runners can continue on the 3-mile Neponset River Greenway trail (see p. 126), which ends near the Central Ave. Red Line station.

HarborWalk One-Way, Section 3: Pleasure Bay to UMASS Boston

Thompson Island

Pleasure Bay

Dorchester Bay

Fort Independence Park

Fort Independence

Pleasure Bay Park

Marine Park

Farragut Rd

City Point

Independence Square Park

Christopher's Rec Playground

E Broadway

Summer St

L St

William J Day Blvd

Dorchester Heights

Thomas Park

Dorchester St

Dorchester Heights Nat'l Hist' Site

W Broadway

W 1st St

E 8th St

Babe Ruth Rd

Columbia Rd

Columbus Park

Carson Beach

Carson Beach

John F Kennedy Library and Museum

University Of Massachusetts-Boston

HarborWalk Path

HarborWalk Path

HarborWalk Path

HarborWalk Path

Bayside Expo Center

Morrissey Blvd

Savin Hill

Boston Globe

Old Colony Ave

Columbia Rd

Columbia Rd

Preble St

D St

Colony Ave

W 1st St

Dorchester St

Dorchester Ave

Dorchester Ave

Boston St

Frontage Rd

Southampton St

Southampton St

Old Colony Ave

Mass Ave Conn

Wareham St

Albany St

Lucy's Playground

CTR

William Eustis Playground

Robert F Ryan Play Area

Savin Hill Ave

Uphams Corner

8

6.8

9

10

11

12

12.7

LEGEND

Start/End

Route/Direction

1   Mile Marker

N   North

HarborWalk Downtown Loop:
North Station to Fort Point Channel and Back

ESSENTIALS		
DISTANCE **7.0** Miles *with many options for a longer or shorter route*	**STARTING POINT**	North Station
	TERRAIN	Flat. Surface around Burroughs Wharf can be muddy. Parts not maintained in winter.
	LIGHTING	Good along "road" sections, and some parts of HarborWalk path are lit at night
	BATHROOMS	Public toilets at USS Constitution Museum, Long Wharf, Aquarium
	WATER	USS Constitution Museum in Charlestown, Aquarium
	PUBLIC TRANSPORTATION	Numerous T stops downtown; Silver Line on waterfront
	PARKING	Parking meters and public parking lots
	ADDITIONAL SPURS	See other HarborWalk sections and spurs, p. 53-75

Overview

This route features the 3.5-mile section of the HarborWalk from North Station to Fort Point channel and back. The first part of the run, until approximately the Aquarium, does a lot of darting to and from the water and up and down piers, due to the geography of the area and the fact that some waterfront areas are still not accessible to the public. Runners should be attentive to the directions. The run starts at a new, unsigned boardwalk that goes from North Station to the North End HarborWalk path, and along a pretty section with excellent ocean views. From Mirabella Pool to Long Wharf, the run flirts with the water and Commercial St., up and down several piers. The view from Burroughs Wharf is especially rewarding. Once at Long Wharf, the route is fairly seamless along the water, with clear signage along most sections. My favorite parts of this area are Rowes Wharf and the spectacular archway of the Boston Harbor Hotel with views to downtown, and the path on the outside of the Moakley Federal Courthouse and the newly completed sections around the Institute of Contemporary Art and Fan Pier. The return retraces the route to North Station, although for variety and a slightly shorter run back there is a option to take the Rose Kennedy Greenway (see p. 69).

START: North Station T Station at Causeway St. and Canal St.

0.0 **PROCEED EAST** along Causeway St., briefly, to Beverly St. Ext. just after the TD Bank North Garden.

LEFT on Beverly St. Ext., **BRIEFLY** to the parking lot on the right at 131 Beverly St. at Lovejoy Wharf.

GET ONTO RAMP, *(no HW sign)*, going underneath Charlestown Bridge, to North End section of HW. Nice views of Zakim Bridge.

CONTINUE on HW path, along water, to Commercial St. at the Mirabella Pool.

0.4 **SOUTH** (toward downtown) on Commercial St. *(NOTE: very soon there is another HW sign, but the gate is locked)*. Cross Hanover St., to Battery Wharf.

0.6 **LEFT** on Battery St., following HW sign for Burroughs Wharf. Great view.

FOLLOW HW around, exiting Union Wharf through parking lot to Commercial St.

LEFT, proceeding **SOUTH** on Commercial St. *(Turns into Atlantic Ave.)* **LEFT** at Sargent's Wharf, at HW sign, to Lewis Wharf.

EXIT Lewis Wharf to Atlantic Ave.

1.2 **LEFT** on Atlantic Ave., continuing south. Here the seamless HW along the water begins, passing Joe's restaurant at Commercial Wharf, to the intersection of Long Wharf, Christopher Columbus Park, and the Marriott hotel. The park is pleasant and festive, always filled with people.

FOLLOW HW trail, around Long Wharf, to the Aquarium, and to Rowes Wharf.

CONTINUE past Rowes Wharf along the HW, behind the Boston Harbor Hotel and the domed walkway with a view to downtown. Just after hotel, see the Northern Ave. Pedestrian Bridge.

2.2 **LEFT** onto Northern Ave. Bridge, at famous James Hook Lobster Co. **CONTINUE ALONG HW** around the Federal Courthouse building, then along the wonderful Fan Pier section, to the new Institute of Contemporary Art.

2.7 **GO AROUND** the outside of the ICA, staying on the water, to Putnam Plaza, at Anthony's Pier 4 restaurant. Come out onto Seaport Blvd.

LEFT on Seaport Blvd., briefly, to the Seaport World Trade Center sign.

3.0 **LEFT** at the Seaport WTC sign (Dunkin' Donuts), following the 1/2-mile loop around Commonwealth Pier, with nice water views. Come back out to Seapoint Blvd./Northern Ave.

3.5 **END** of one way.

RETRACE ROUTE to North Station.

7.0 **END**

See page 69 for Fort Point Channel spur options.

HarborWalk Downtown Loop: N. Station to Fort Point Channel and Back

Langone Recreational Complex

US Coast Guard Station

Charlestown Brg (walk)

N. Washington St

Charter St

Commercial St

Callahan Tunl

Old North Church

Hull St

Salem St

Tileston St

Prince St

Endicott St

Battery St

Clark St

Fleet St

Hanover St

Richmond St

North St

Union Wharf

Paul Revere House

Lewis Wharf

Commercial Wharf

Cooper St

Hillman St

Cross St

Atlantic Ave

Commercial St

Christopher Columbus Park

Long Whrf

Clinton St

Faneuil Hall Marketplace

North St

Holocaust Memorial Park

New England Aquarium

Government Center At Scollay Square

Congress St

Chatham St

State St

Boston City Hall

Boston Old City Hall

Killby St

Broad St

Milk St

Water St

School St

John F Fitzgerald Surface Rd

Post Office Square Park

Broad St

Rowes Wharf

Milk St

Franklin St

Oliver St

Moakley Courthouse

Orpheum Theatre

Devonshire St

Federal St

High St

Pearl St

ICA

Commonwealth Pier

New England Telephone Building

Purchase St

Atlantic Ave

N. Ave. Ped Bridge

Courthouse Way

Northern Ave

Arch St

Otis St

Summer St

Bedford St

Federal Reserve Bank

Boston Tea Party Ship And Museum

Seaport Blvd

Sleeper St

Essex St

John F Fitzgerald Surface Rd

Lincoln St

South St

Utica St

Atlantic Ave

Dorchester Ave

Children's Museum Of Boston

Congress St

Summer St

Farnsworth St

Thomson Pl

Stillings St

Boston Wharf Rd

E Service Rd

B St

Seaport World Trade Center

Boston Fish Pier

Turnaround

Northern Ave

Amtrak-Boston South Station

Necco St

Congress St

World Trade Center Ave

Seaport Blvd

Park Ln

Necco Ct

Binford St

W Service Rd Ext

W Side Dr

A St

Channel Center St

Medallion Rd

Bypass Rd

Congress St

Boston Convention & Exhibition Ctr

Inman St

Fargo St

Channel St

D St

Gillette

LEGEND

Start/End

Route/Direction

1 Mile Marker

N North

HarborWalk Downtown Loop:
Charlestown Spur (2.4 mile add-on)

Overview

This run adds onto the HarborWalk Downtown Loop with a 2.4 mile spur to Charlestown and back, for a total distance of 9.5 miles. The Charlestown section of the HarborWalk is accessible and enjoyable, featuring a combination of waterfront views and historic sites. Highlights include the new Paul Revere Park, the fascinating and scenic area around the USS Constitution, and the expanded HarborWalk path through the Charlestown Navy Yard and its many interesting and historic buildings. For further details on Charlestown sights and route options, please see the "Historic Charlestown Run" on p. 21.

Distance Directions

START: North Station at "T" Station at Canal St.

0.0 **PROCEED EAST** along Causeway St., briefly, to Beverly St. Ext.

LEFT on Beverly St. Ext., straight through to the Police Marine Division parking lot, to a "floating" walkway crossing over the water to Charlestown.

CROSS OVER WATER along floating walkway. *(Caution: surface is slippery and narrow.)*

0.3 **ENTER** the new Paul Revere Park.

HEAD RIGHT out of the park, along Constitution Rd. in front of the Marriott hotel, past the Constitution Landing sign, and past the gate, to Constitution Wharf, and the USS Constitution Museum.

Detour Options: Lovely ¼ mile HW spur behind the Marriott Hotel, around the Marina. It ends abruptly at a gate so you will have to double back. Also, numerous opportunities to run down a couple of the piers, each of which is circa 0.3m each way.

0.8 At the USS Constitution Museum, follow HW sign on the east side of the pier (closest to museum). Terrific views here.

1.1 Pier 6, Tavern on the Water restaurant.

CONTINUE following HW signs, past piers 6,7,8. Interesting buildings and interpretive signs here. HW trail ends at intersection of 16th St. and 1st Ave.

1.7 **TURN UP** 16th St., briefly, and then **LEFT** on 2nd Ave.

LEFT on 2nd Ave., which is a pedestrian mall in parts. Go up stairs, alongside building, then back down stairs, to path.

FOLLOW 2nd Ave. back to the USS Constitution Museum.

2.2 **RETURN** to Paul Revere Park, then back over the floating walkway
at New Charles River Basin sign on the brick building.

Now you are back at the Police Marine Division parking lot.

PROCEED BRIEFLY to the parking lot on the left. There is a small ramp,
NO SIGN, but look for 131 Beverly St. building.

2.4 **END.**

RETURN to N. Station or **CONTINUE** HarborWalk Loop run (page 63),
at ramp going under Charlestown Bridge (no sign).

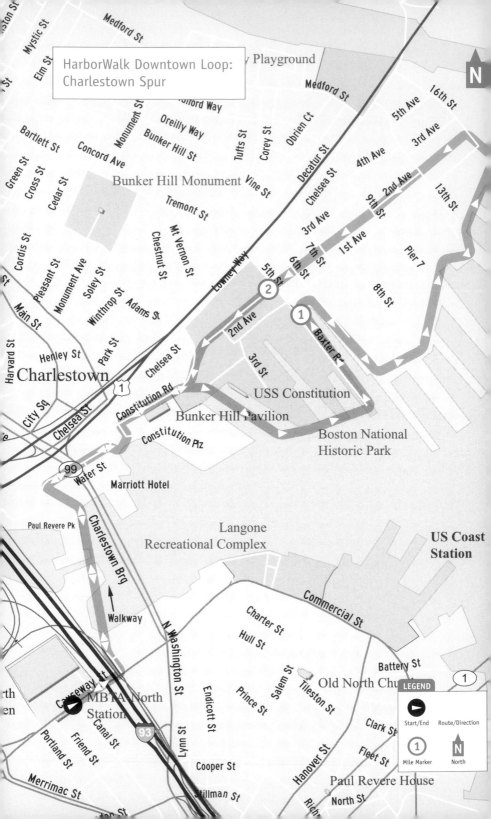

HarborWalk Downtown Loop: Charlestown Spur

Mystic St
Medford St
Elm St
Mystic St
Playground
Medford St
N

Bartlett St
Concord Ave
Medford Way
Oreilly Way
Bunker Hill St
Tufts St
Corey St
Obrien Ct
Decatur St
5th Ave
16th St
3rd Ave

Green St
Cross St
Cedar St
Bunker Hill Monument
Vine St
Chelsea St
4th Ave
2nd Ave
9th St
13th St

Tremont St
3rd Ave
1st Ave
Pier 7

Cordis St
Pleasant St
Monument Ave
Soley St
Winthrop St
Adams St
Mt Vernon St
Chestnut St
Lomey Way
5th St
6th St
7th St
8th St

Main St
Park St
2nd Ave
1

Harvard St
Henley St
Chelsea St
3rd St
Baxter R.

Charlestown
Constitution Rd
USS Constitution

City Sq
Chelsea St
Constitution Plz
Bunker Hill Pavilion
Boston National Historic Park

99
Water St
Marriott Hotel

Paul Revere Pk
Charlestown Brg
Langone Recreational Complex
US Coast Station

Walkway
Commercial St

North Station
N Washington St
Charter St
Hull St
Salem St
Tileston St
Old North Chu
Battery St
1

MBTA North Station
Prince St
Endicott St
Clark St

Canal St
Friend St
93
Lynn St
Cooper St
Hanover St
Fleet St

Portland St
Merrimac St
Hillman St
North St
Paul Revere House

LEGEND
Start/End   Route/Direction
1 Mile Marker   N North

HarborWalk Downtown Loop:
Fort Point Channel Spur and Rose Kennedy Greenway Return

Overview

An additional spur of the HarborWalk has evolved over the past couple of years, featuring the Fort Point Channel area. A beautiful public walkway behind the new Intercontinental Hotel is the gateway to a well-marked 1-mile section of the HarborWalk, crossing the water over the Congress St. Bridge to the Children's Museum and continuing along the Fort Point Channel, ending at the Gillette Building. There are some small parks and interesting signs and features along the way. The return, instead of repeating the entire HW path back to North Station, uses the Rose Kennedy Greenway, which runs 1.2 miles from South Station to North Station. The Greenway is a pedestrian-friendly and direct way to run or walk through the heart of downtown, along what used to be the Central Artery highway. There are numerous small parks, fountains, public art, and other interesting sights along this still-evolving 25-acre open space.

This spur starts at the turnaround point of the HarborWalk Downtown Loop Run (page 63), at Commonwealth Pier. Instead of retracing your steps the 3.5 miles back to North Station, runners will add the approximately 2-mile Fort Point Channel spur, and then return to North Station via the Rose Kennedy Greenway. This would make the total run 7.3 miles (8.7 miles if the Charlestown spur is added). The overall distance is less than one would think because the Rose Kennedy Greenway route through downtown is so direct!

Directions

Distance

START: Commonwealth Pier, Seaport Blvd. & WTC Drive (Dunkin' Donuts)

NOTE: If you came from North Station along the HW, you would be at 3.5 miles and if you added the Charlestown loop you would be at 5.9 miles, assuming you have done the 0.5m loop around Commonwealth pier.

0.0 Follow **HW PATH NORTH** around the ICA, Fan Pier, the Federal Courthouse, and then over the Northern Ave. Pedestrian Bridge. As you cross the bridge, see the new Intercontinental Hotel across the way, at Independence Wharf (470 Atlantic Ave.).

Note: If you want to run just the Fort Point Channel spur, start at Independence Wharf.

0.9 Cross onto HW path behind the Intercontinental Hotel. Good HW signs in this area. Continue to Congress St. Bridge.

CROSS Congress St. Bridge, to the Boston Children's Museum and Hood Milk Bottle.

1.2 **GO DOWN STAIRS** on the south side of the Congress St. Bridge, opposite the Milk Bottle, following the water.

COME BACK UP STAIRS, onto the Summer St. Bridge, and, immediately cross the street, see another set of stairs adjacent to Melcher St.

GO DOWN STAIRS, and run along the HW path, with Fort Point Channel on your right. Continue to the end of the path, at the Gillette Building and the intersection with Dorchester Ave. and the Post Office building. Pedestrians are not permitted to enter the east side of the Fort Point Channel, so steps must be retraced.

1.8 **RETRACE STEPS** on the HarborWalk path, returning to the Summer St. Bridge.

2.3 **LEFT** on the Summer St. Bridge, past South Station, to the intersection with the Rose Kennedy Greenway.

2.6 **RIGHT** on the Rose Kennedy Greenway, which goes over the newly depressed central artery. There are good pedestrian crossings along the way.

CONTINUE on the Rose Kennedy Greenway, crossing Congress St., Seaport Blvd., State St., and Hanover St., to Causeway St. (*Note: the crossing after Hanover St. is a little tricky*).

3.8 **END,** at Causeway St.

7.3 **TOTAL** without Charlestown Spur.

9.7 **TOTAL** with Charlestown Spur.

HarborWalk Downtown Loop:
Fort Point Channel Spur with
Rose Kennedy Greenway Return

South Bay Beauty:
HarborWalk and More in South Boston

ESSENTIALS

DISTANCE		
Various options, from 5 to 10 miles	**STARTING POINT**	Head Island Causeway at Pleasure Bay
	TERRAIN	Flat as a pancake; almost entirely off-road
	LIGHTING	Quite good
	BATHROOMS	Head Island Playground, Carson Beach (seasonal)
	WATER	Head Island Playground, Carson Beach (seasonal)
	INTERESTING SITES	Pleasure Bay, Fort Independence, Carson Beach, JFK Library, UMass Boston
	PUBLIC TRANSPORTATION	Red Line/Commuter Rail: JFK/UMASS station
	PARKING	Ample parking along route

Overview

This is the longest, most seamless, and accessible oceanfront path in Boston. Much of the run is off-road, following the continually improving south section of the HarborWalk. This run is worth going out of one's way to get to, as there are spectacular water views nearly the entire way. The run starts along Head Island Causeway, a paved off-road path looping around Pleasure Bay, featuring great views of Logan Airport and a tour of Fort Independence on Castle Island. Returning to Day Blvd., you'll then head along City Beach, to the McCormack Bath House at Carson Beach, where the short run turns back. From Carson Beach is a spectacular boardwalk trail to the JFK Library, which features interpretive maps, beautiful rotundas, and fabulous views of the water and Boston skyline. After heading around the JFK Library, continue the final mile along the HaborWalk around Dorchester Bay with beautiful views to Fox point, to the end at UMASS Boston. In the summer, there are snack bars at Castle Island and Carson Beach. The beaches are safe for swimming. This run is especially a treat at sunrise, as it faces east.

There are three main options for this run. The short route, at a little over 5 miles, leads from Pleasure Bay to Carson beach and back. The medium run is nearly 8 miles, adding 1.3 miles each way out to the JFK Library. The long run adds a mile out to the UMASS Boston campus, to clock in at nearly 10 miles total.

If you want to add even more, it is a (not very pleasant) 1.6 miles from UMASS Boston to the northern terminus of the (very pleasant) 3-mile Neponset River Greenway. You can run to the south end of the trail at the Central Ave. Red Line station and take the "T" back. See p. 126 for the entire Neponset River Greenway run.

START: Head Island Causeway and William Day Blvd. Ample parking.

SHORT RUN: Pleasure Bay Loop to McCormack Bath House at Carson Beach and
              Return: 5.3 miles

0.0   Start by running around the perimeter of Pleasure Bay, on Head Island
       Causeway. You will go by Fort Independence Park and on Castle Island,
       a playground and a beach. Return to the intersection of Day Blvd. and
       Head Island Causeway.

2.1   **SOUTH** along William Day Blvd., with water on your left. City Beach,
       the L Street Bath House, and several Yacht Clubs will be on your left.
       Continue for a little over 1.5 miles to McCormack Bath House at Carson
       Beach (snack bar, public restrooms).

       NOTE: HW path breaks off from Day Blvd. opposite Moakley Park.

3.7   **TURN AROUND** at the Bath House, retracing your steps to the intersec-
       tion of Head Island and William Day Blvd.

5.3   **END**

MEDIUM RUN: Pleasure Bay Loop to JFK Library and RETURN: 7.9 miles
This loop adds 2.6 miles to the Short Run (1.3m each way).

3.7   **CONTINUE** past Carson Beach, following main pathway along water.
       The JFK Library is ahead.

       *NOTE: The path does not continue exactly to the JFK Library. Just before
       the library, proceed right, off the path and up a hill. There is a worn foot-
       path here. Go over the hill, and continue down to the Library and re-enter
       the path. Continue around, to the other side of the Library and dock with
       great views of Dorchester Bay.*

5.0   **RETURN** to the McCormack Bath House.

6.3   **RETURN** to Head Island and William Day Blvd. intersection.

7.9   **END**

LONG RUN: Pleasure Bay Loop to UMASS Boston and Back: 9.7 miles
*This loop adds 4.4 miles to the Short Run (2.2m each way) and 1.8 miles to
the Medium Run (0.9m each way).*

Follow Medium Run from dock at JFK Library, continuing south.

5.0   **CONTINUE SOUTH** from JFK Library, along the HarborWalk pathway
       south to UMASS Boston. There are great views out to Dorchester Bay
       on the left, with the UMASS campus and state Archives building on
       the right. Stay on the path until the intersection with Rt. 3A/Morrissey
       Blvd.

5.9   **TURN AROUND,** retracing steps northward to Head Island Causeway,
       and William Day Blvd. intersection.

9.7   **END**

South Bay Beauty (South Boston HarborWalk) Sections

Section	Segment Distance	Total Distance
Starting at Head Island Causeway and William Day Blvd.		
Head Island Causeway loop	2.1	2.1
Day Blvd./Causeway to McCormack Bath House	1.6	3.7
McCormack Bath House to JFK Library Dock	1.3	5.0
JFK Library Dock to UMASS Boston at Rt. 3A	0.9	5.9

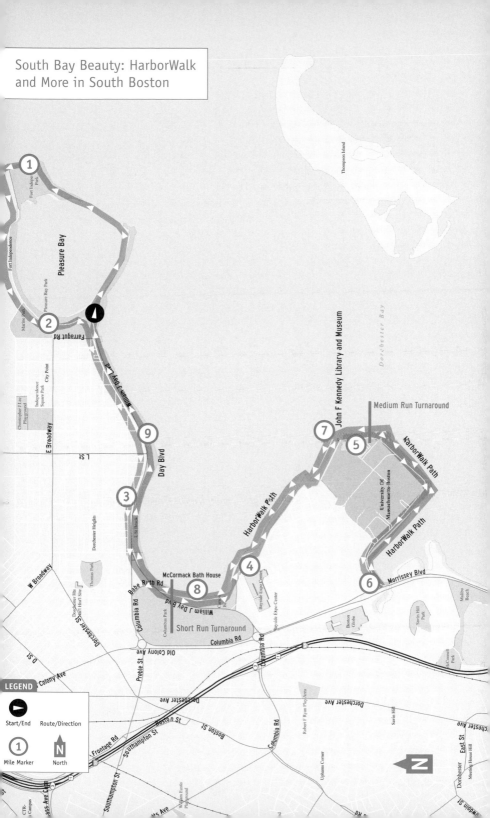

South Bay Beauty: HarborWalk and More in South Boston

Ocean Spectacular:
Deer Island and Winthrop Shore Drive

ESSENTIALS		
DISTANCE **7** Miles; Deer Island only is 2.6 miles	**STARTING POINT**	Deer Island Parking Lot, Point Shirley
	TERRAIN	Flat, but hill options on Deer Island
	LIGHTING	Deer Island path not lit at night
	BATHROOMS	Visitor Center on Deer Island
	WATER	Visitor Center on Deer Island
	INTERESTING SITES	Great views of the city; Fascinating history of Deer Island, with good interpretive maps; Visitor Center
	PUBLIC TRANSPORTATION	Not easy to get to Deer Island via public transportation. Nearest T station is Orient Heights.
	PARKING	Parking lot at the entrance to Deer Island

Overview

Here is an opportunity to run nearly 7 miles along the ocean, much of it off road and with little traffic. The run starts at Deer Island, which offers the fascinating contrast of existing as a $4 billion space-age wastewater treatment plant and spectacular area for running. The 2.6-mile path goes around a 60-acre park, featuring great views of the harbor and Boston skyline, and a dramatic 15-story egg-shaped treatment plant. There are numerous interpretive signs along the run, and a terrific Visitor Center, where great detail is available about the technology of the treatment facility. The highest point on the island, at 135 feet, offers great views of the entire harbor, Winthrop, and the Boston skyline. At the island's southern tip, a small lighthouse can be seen 400 yards into the harbor. There are memorials to Irish immigrants who were quarantined on Deer Island in the mid-1800s. Deer Island was also the site of a series of penal institutions, the last of which closed in 1991.

Runners can add to the 2.6 mile Deer Island loop with a run along Winthrop Shore Drive. This adds 2.2 miles each way to the run, making for a total of 7 miles. Though there are water views along much of Winthrop Shore Drive, there are a couple of sections that go "inland" and the layout and signage can be a little confusing.

START: Parking lot at Point Shirley, at entrance to Deer Island perimeter path.

0.0 From parking lot, follow signs for the perimeter path. Follow the perimeter path around Deer Island. It is 2.6 miles around. *Note there are some additional options to run up and along the hill.*

2.6 **END DEER ISLAND LOOP**

To take the Shore Drive spur:
(Note: signs can be sparse and the layout of the area is a little confusing.)

2.6 Take Tafts Ave. out from the Deer Island parking lot, to intersection with Shirley St.

2.9 **RIGHT** on Shirley St., going by Coughlin Park on the left, to Moore St.

3.7 **RIGHT** on Moore St., briefly to Winthrop Shore Drive.

3.8 **LEFT** on Winthrop Shore Drive. Follow almost exactly 1 mile, to end at Rt. 145 just after Locust St. This is enjoyable for running, with water views along a good part of the way.

4.8 **TURN AROUND** just after Locust St.

RETRACE STEPS to Deer Island Parking lot, along Winthrop Shore Drive.

Option: Run on Shore Drive out and Shirley St. back, for variety.

7.0 **END**

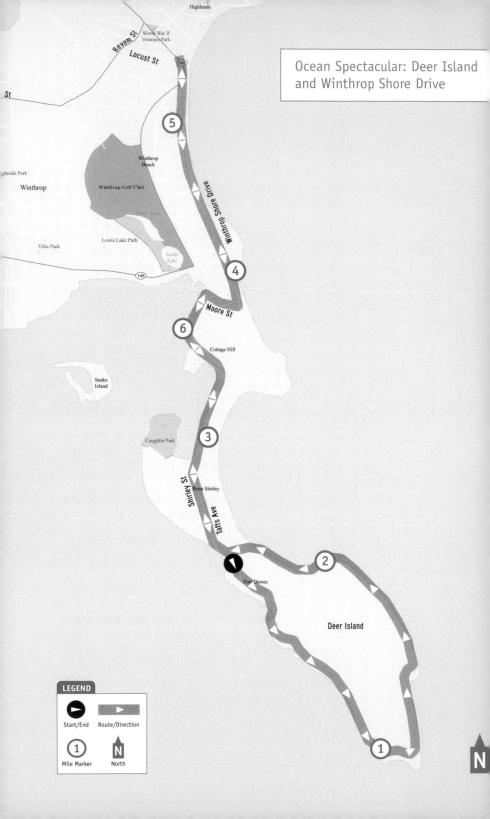

Ocean Spectacular: Deer Island and Winthrop Shore Drive

From Piers to Parks: East Boston Greenway, Piers Park, Harborside Drive

ESSENTIALS		
DISTANCE **5.2** Miles; *Over 10 miles with Bell Isle Marsh extension*	**STARTING POINT**	Bremen St., opposite Airport T Station, Blue Line
	TERRAIN	Flat
	LIGHTING	Not all paths are lit at night
	BATHROOMS	Bremen St. Park, T Station, Hyatt Hotel
	WATER	Bremen St. Park, Piers Park
	INTERESTING SITES	Great views of the city; Piers Park, on the ocean; Bremen Street Park; Harborside drive
	PUBLIC TRANSPORTATION	Blue Line T stations – Airport, Maverick
	ADDITIONAL SPUR	Bell Isle Marsh and Constitution Beach, p. 84

Overview

East Boston is an overlooked area for runners and walkers. Enormous changes and improvements have occurred there over the past several years. As part of the Big Dig mitigation, several new parks and the still-evolving linear park called the East Boston Greenway have been built. A quick drive through the tunnel or ride on the Blue Line will reward runners with a run that is nearly all off-road, with spectacular water and city views, and a jaunt through the new and unique Bremen Street Park. And, if by chance you're stuck at Logan and can find a way to stash your stuff, this is an easily accessible way to kill some time. Maybe we can convince MassPort to put a locker room and showers at the airport!

This run, just short of five miles, starts at the Airport "T" on the new East Boston Greenway linear park. About 1.5 miles of a planned 3 miles of the path are completed. After taking the eastern part of the path to the end, a few side streets will take you to Piers Park, which is a beautifully designed spot right on the water and a terrific place to take in some views. Come back up the "magic stairs", getting onto the East Boston section of the HarborWalk, which features great views of the water, airport, and city, as you run by the Hyatt Harborside hotel. For the return, rejoin the East Boston Greenway, enjoying Bremen Street Park, which features a community garden, playground, splash pool in the summer, amphitheater for performances, and a bocce court. An additional spur section of the Greenway features a nice loop around Memorial Stadium.

One special treat for the end of the run is a detour to Santarpio's Pizza — an institution and arguably the best pizza in the city.

START: Bremen St., opposite Airport T Station

0.0 Come out of the Airport T station along a path that leads to Bremen Street Park.

LEFT on the path, heading toward the city, airport and water (not toward Winthrop). You will go under several underpasses, where murals have been painted by students from City Year, Zumix, and the Youth Conservation Corps.

0.4 Maverick St. underpass. In the summer, beautiful flowers along this section.

0.5 Sumner St. underpass.

0.7 **END** of EBG path at Marginal St., at a blue caboose. Just ahead is a fence, with a "Gate C" sign where some new condos are going to be built.

LEFT on Marginal St., getting off path. You will soon see an opportunity to get off Marginal St., going down to Piers Point Park.

RUN AROUND Pier 3 at Piers Point Park, then back up to Marginal St.

GO UP STAIRS, called the "Golden Stairs", which connect Marginal St. to Webster St.

1.3 **RIGHT** on Webster St. to the intersection with Jeffries St.

1.6 **RIGHT** on Jeffries St., to Marginal St.

SEE HarborWalk signs. **ENTER** HarborWalk path and follow all the way around to the end. This is a spectacular section along the water, with great views of the water, the Boston skyline, and planes coming into Logan Airport. The path parallels Harborside Dr., going past the Hyatt Hotel at the airport.

2.4 **TURN AROUND** at end and return 0.5 miles along the HarborWalk and intersection with Maverick St.

2.9 **LEFT** on Maverick St., to Venice St.

3.2 **RIGHT** on Venice St., to Porter St.

LEFT on Porter St., briefly, to a park with numerous paths.

TAKE PERIMETER PATH, COUNTERCLOCKWISE around Memorial Stadium and an athletic field.

4.2 **REJOIN** Greenway, at Bremen St. Park

RIGHT on Greenway path, heading toward Winthrop, through Bremen St. Park, to end of park.

CONTINUE along pathway at end of park, past Prescott St., to the end of the path.

NOTE: There is a gate at the end of the park that is sometimes closed, so you might have to turn around here.

4.8 **TURN AROUND,** and return on the path to the middle of the park and the Airport T Station.

5.2 **END** at Bremen St. Park and Airport T Station.

See page 84 for additional spur to Constitution Beach and Bell Isle Marsh.

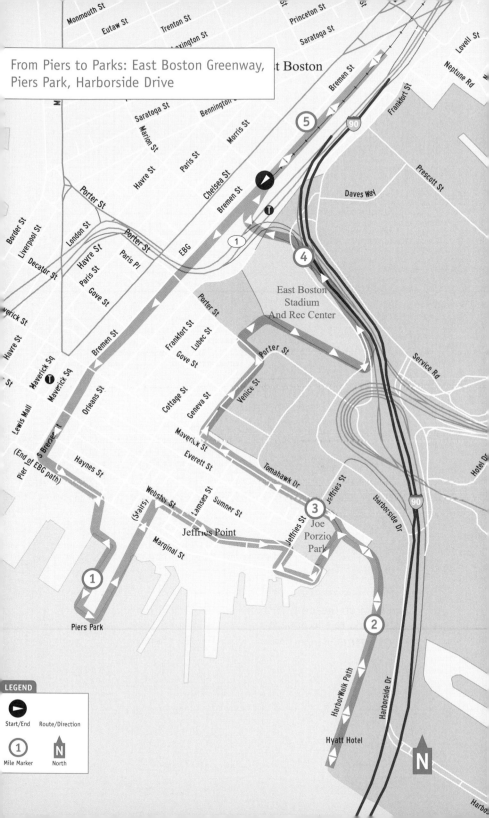

From Piers to Parks: East Boston Greenway, Piers Park, Harborside Drive

East Boston

Monmouth St
Eutaw St
Trenton St
Lexington St
Princeton St
Saratoga St
Lovell St
Neptune Rd

Saratoga St
Bennington St
Bremen St
Frankfort St
Prescott St

Marion St
Morris St
Daves Way

Paris St
Chelsea St
Bremen St

Porter St
EBG

Border St
Liverpool St
London St
Havre St
Paris Pl
Porter St

Decatur St
Havre St
Paris St
Gove St

Bremen St
Porter St
East Boston Stadium And Rec Center

Frankfort St
Lubec St
Gove St
Venice St
Porter St
Service Rd

Maverick Sq
Orleans St
Cottage St
Geneva St
Maverick St
Tomahawk Dr

Lewis Mall
Haynes St
Everett St
Jeffries St
Jeffries St

(End of EBG path)
Pier of EBG path
(Stairs)
Webster St
Lamson St
Sumner St
Jeffries Point
Joe Porzio Park

Marginal St
Harborside Dr

Piers Park
HarborWalk Path
Harborside Dr

Hyatt Hotel

LEGEND

Start/End   Route/Direction

Mile Marker   North

N

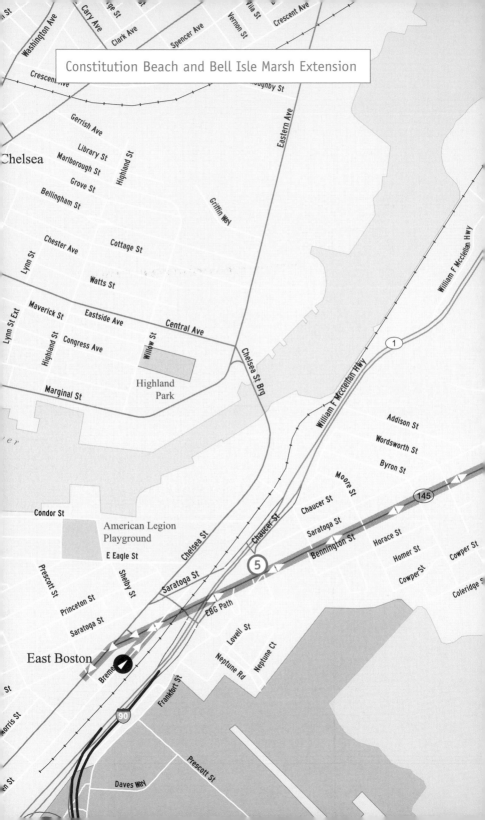

Constitution Beach and Bell Isle Marsh Extension

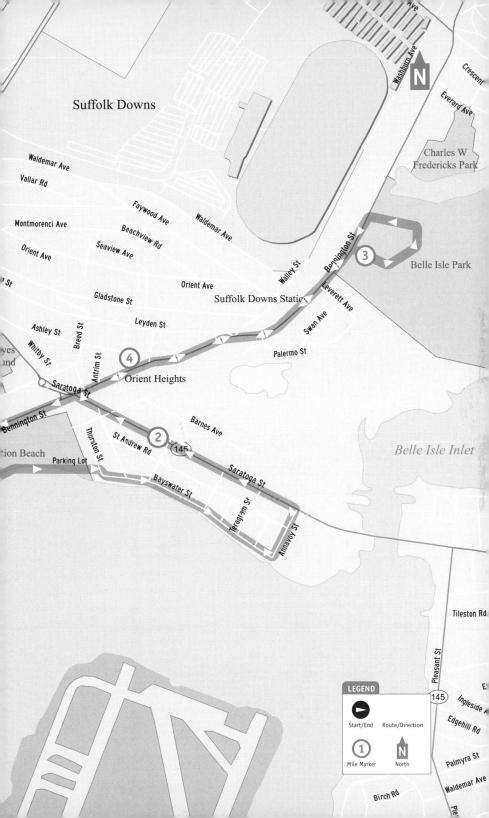

Suffolk Downs

Waldemar Ave

Vallar Rd

Montmorenci Ave

Orient Ave

Faywood Ave

Beachview Rd

Seaview Ave

Waldemar Ave

Walley St

Bennington St

3

Belle Isle Park

Charles W Fredericks Park

Crescent

Everard Ave

Washburn Ave

N

Orient Ave

Gladstone St

Leyden St

Suffolk Downs Station

Leverett Ave

Swan Ave

Ashley St

Breed St

Whitby St

Antrim St

Saratoga St

4

Orient Heights

Palermo St

Bennington St

Thurston St

St Andrew Rd

Barnes Ave

2

145

Saratoga St

Belle Isle Inlet

Parking Lot

Bayswater St

Teragram St

Annavoy St

Tileston Rd

Pleasant St

145

Ingleside

Edgehill Rd

Palmyra St

Waldemar Ave

Birch Rd

LEGEND

Start/End   Route/Direction

1
Mile Marker   North   N

Constitution Beach and Bell Isle Marsh Extension

For those wanting a longer run, add a spur out to Constitution Beach and Bell Isle Marsh. There are a couple of less pleasant sections through busy and congested roads, but the reward is a mile-long waterfront run along Constitution Beach and Bayswater St., and then the winding pathways of 241-acre Bell Isle Marsh, which is one of Boston's largest surviving salt marshes. The Marsh is a favorite of birders, and has a nice set of walking paths and boardwalks, leading to a fire tower with a great view. Bennington St./Rt. 145, which is the main connector to the beach and marsh, is a main road with lots of traffic but there is a good sidewalk and a marked bike lane on the road.

Distance Directions

START: Bremen St. Park at Airport T Station.

0.0   East Boston Greenway Path toward Winthrop, alongside Bremen St., to the intersection with Bennington St. (**DO NOT** exit the park for the last little bit of the EBG to Prescott St.)

        RIGHT on Bennington St./Rt. 145, about 1 mile to a sign for Constitution Beach and an overpass.

1.0   **TAKE THE OVERPASS**, onto Constitution Beach. A beautiful view opens up. **LEFT** at Constitution Beach, as you face the water, through the paved parking lot.

1.3   **RIGHT** on Bayswater St. Continue on Bayswater, at the Orient Heights Yacht Club, to the end at Annavoy St.

        LEFT at Annavoy St., to end, returning to Rt. 145, which is now Saratoga St.

1.9   **LEFT** on Saratoga St. This is less pleasant for running, but needed to connect to Bell Isle Marsh.

2.3   **RIGHT** on Bennington St., passing the Orient Heights T Station, to entrance to Bell Isle Marsh right after crossing Leverett Ave.

3.0   **ENTER** Bell Isle Marsh. There is a series of winding pathways here, leading to a terrific ocean view from an observation tower. Bell Isle Marsh is a favorite of birders. *Note: We have not specifically routed Bell Isle Marsh but we assume about 0.5 miles. The path can be occasionally muddy.*

3.5   **EXIT** Bell Isle Marsh.

        LEFT on Bennington St. (Rt. 145). Follow Bennington St. all the way back to the intersection with Bremen St. and the Airport T station.

5.6   **END**

NOTE: For those wanting to do the entire East Boston Greenway path, Piers Park, HarborWalk, and Bell Isle extension, and save 3 miles, take the T to Suffolk Downs, and start the run at Bell Isle Marsh. Then run back to the EBG path and do the Piers Park and HaborWalk section, ending the run at the Airport T station.

Harbor Island Jaunt:
Spectacle Island

ESSENTIALS		
DISTANCE *No specific route*	**STARTING POINT**	Ferry station on Long Wharf (Aquarium Blue Line)
	TERRAIN	Gently hilly. Trails not maintained in winter.
	LIGHTING	Not open at night.
	BATHROOMS	Public toilet on Long Wharf, public restroom at Spectacle Island Visitor Center
	WATER	Spectacle Island Visitor Center
	INTERESTING SITES	All of the island is interesting; great views of the water and Boston skyline; 2.5-mile interpretive tour

Overview

The Boston Harbor Islands National Park, established in 1996, features 34 islands, and over 35 miles of undeveloped shoreline, all within ten miles of downtown Boston. Spectacle Island, which was "reborn" as a park out of the clay and sediment from the Big Dig project, is the best of the Harbor Islands for running. The island features about 5 miles of dirt trails, over rolling hills, with great views of the water and the Boston skyline. The highest point is 176 feet. A Visitor Center at the ferry landing on Spectacle Island features a café, restrooms, water, and, on Sundays in the summer, outdoor jazz concerts. Along the paths, there are interpretive signs, shade pavilions, picnic tables, and wonderful view points.

Spectacle Island is twelve minutes by ferry from Long Wharf (Aquarium I Station, Blue Line). Ferries run about every hour to and from the island from early May to mid-October, and then on weekends until early November. Note that ferries do not run to Spectacle Island from November through April. Consult the Boston Harbor Islands web site, bostonharborislands.org, for detailed information about the islands, ferry schedules and fares.

There is not a specific running "route" in this book for Spectacle Island. I recommend you use the accompanying map, which shows a series of trails and island highlights, to plan your own romp around the island. The map also contains a 2.5-mile self-guided tour, with interpretive signs.

Note: Deer Island, one of the National Park islands that is accessible by land, is featured as a separate run in this book, on page 76.

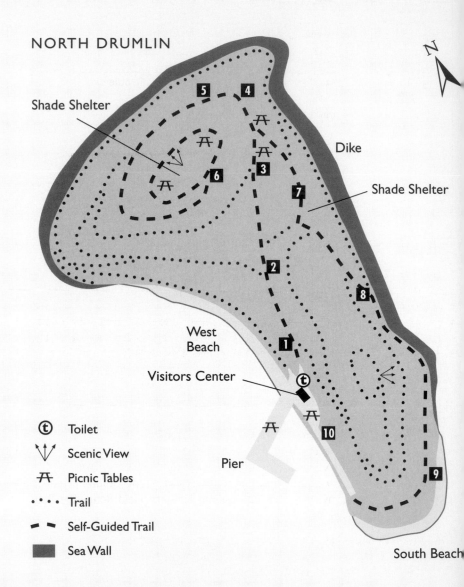

Harbor Island Jaunt:
Spectacle Island

NORTH DRUMLIN

Shade Shelter

Dike

Shade Shelter

West
Beach

Visitors Center

Pier

ⓣ Toilet

⋁ Scenic View

⊼ Picnic Tables

• • • • Trail

— — Self-Guided Trail

▬ Sea Wall

South Beach

Courtesy: Massachusetts Department of Conservation and Recreation

The Charles River Paths

ESSENTIALS		
DISTANCE *Various options*	**STARTING POINT**	Multiple Access Points available. Best cross-overs to the river are at Charles/MGH, Fiedler Bridge at Arlington St. & Beacon St., and Harvard Bridge at Mass. Ave
	TERRAIN	Almost entirely flat
	LIGHTING	Good in some spots, not good in others. Not maintained in winter.
	BATHROOMS	Near Fiedler Pedestrian bridge/Hatch Shell
	WATER	A couple of spots near the Hatch Shell
	INTERESTING SITES	Crew teams in the early morning, sailboats on nice evenings. Great views of Boston from Cambridge side, of MIT from Boston side. Historic Longfellow Bridge; Hatch Shell; Museum of Science.

Overview

The Charles River path is one of the great runs in the United States. It is the first place to which hotels direct visitors looking for a place to run. The paths are always festive, with a constant flow of runners, walkers, bikers, bladers, and any other type of "er" you can think of. Early in the morning you'll see crew teams, and on a nice evening in season, a panoply of sailboats on the water. There is a running path on both the Cambridge and Boston side of the river, although it is better developed and maintained on the Boston side. There are great views of the Boston skyline from the Cambridge side and of Cambridge/MIT from the Boston side. The best way to experience the river run is to plot a "loop", incorporating Boston and Cambridge, using one of the several bridge options to cross back over. Some of the highlights of the run, on top of the outstanding views, are the Teddy Ebersol playing fields, the Community Boat House, and the Hatch Memorial Shell. Further up the river, past Harvard Square, there are some very pretty sections, featuring community gardens, the Northeastern University boat house, Charles River Canoe and Paddle, a terrific playground with a spray pool (seasonal) along Soldiers' Field Road, the Daly rink, and Newton Yacht Club.

The Charles River Paths have been recently extended, past Galen St. in Watertown and well into Newton and out to Waltham. Known as the "Upper Charles River Bikeway" loop, it is possible to continue for 6+ miles from Galen St. in Watertown to Norumbega Rd. in Newton, passing through Waltham Center. There are some wonderful, pastoral sections here. This section is not completely seamless and can be a little confusing. There are a few on-road detours and some still incomplete sections, though progress is being made every year.

A very detailed description of the Upper Charles section can be found at a site called the Charles River Bikeway Letterbox:

http://www.geocities.com/haalck@snet.net/charles_river_bikeway_letterbox.htm

Rather than provide a specific running route, several options are presented, with distances between the major sections. The best access sites to the River on the Boston side are: the police station at the intersection of Nashua St. and Storrow Drive, known as Leverett Circle, just after the drawbridge south of the Museum of Science; from Back Bay, via the Arthur Fiedler footbridge, at the intersection of Beacon and Arlington; the pedestrian bridge near the Charles/ MGH "T" station; and further west, at the Harvard Bridge at Mass. Ave.

Segment Distances

Section	Segment Distance	Total Distance
Boston Side		
Police Station @ Leverett Circle to Longfellow Bridge	0.5	0.5
Longfellow Bridge to Harvard Bridge (Mass Ave.)	1.2	1.7
Harvard Bridge to B.U. Bridge	1.1	2.8
B.U. Bridge to River St. Bridge (River St.)	0.9	3.7
River St. Bridge to Western Ave. Bridge	0.2	3.9
Western Ave. Bridge to John Weeks Bridge (pedestrian)	0.3	4.2
J.W. Bridge to Lars Anderson Bridge (N. Harvard/JFK St.) (Harvard Sq.)	0.2	4.4
Lars Anderson Bridge. to Eliot St. Bridge @ Gerry's Landing Blvd. (use underpass to stay on Boston side)	0.5	4.9
Gerry's Landing Blvd. to Arsenal St. Bridge	1.4	6.3
Arsenal St. Bridge to N. Beacon St.	0.7	7.0
N. Beacon St. to Galen St. Nonantum	1.5	8.5

Loop Runs

Below is a series of loop runs, going out progressively further along the river paths, as far as Lars Anderson Bridge in Harvard Square. Each loop starts from the Arthur Fiedler Pedestrian Bridge ramp on the Boston side of Charles River Path, runs along the Boston side of the river, then crosses over the bridge and returns on the Cambridge side, looping back on Rt. 28 past the Museum of Science and the drawbridge at Leverett Circle, returning on the Boston side path to the Fiedler Pedestrian Bridge.

From Fiedler Bridge To:	
Harvard Bridge (Mass. Ave.) Loop	3.75 miles
B.U. Bridge Loop	5.5 miles
Note: to access the B.U. Bridge so it can be crossed over to the Cambridge side, you need to take the footbridge 0.3m east of the B.U., Bridge, then run on Back Rd., to access the stairs going up to the B.U. Bridge.	
River St. Bridge (River St.) Loop	6.9 miles
Weeks Footbridge Loop	8.0 miles
Lars Anderson Bridge (N. Harvard/JFK St.- Harvard Sq.) Loop	8.6 miles

Charles River Loop Distances (miles)

		A	B	C	D	E	F	G	H	I	J	K
A	Mt. Auburn Street	A										
B	North Beacon Street	3.1	B									
C	Arsenal Street	4.6	1.7	C								
D	Eliot Bridge	7.1	4.1	2.6	D							
E	J.F.K. Street	8.7	5.7	4.2	1.8	E						
F	Anderson Footbridge	9.2	6.3	4.7	2.3	0.7	F					
G	Western Avenue	9.8	6.8	5.3	2.9	1.3	0.8	G				
H	River Street	10.2	7.3	5.7	3.3	1.7	1.2	0.8	H			
I	BU Bridge	12.3	9.3	7.8	5.4	3.8	3.3	2.6	2.2	I		
J	Harvard Bridge	14.1	11.2	9.7	7.2	5.6	5.2	4.5	4.1	2.7	J	
K	Longfellow Bridge	16.1	13.2	11.7	9.2	7.6	7.2	6.5	6.1	4.6	2.8	K
L	Leverett Circle	17.1	14.2	12.6	10.2	8.6	8.1	7.5	7.0	5.6	3.8	2.0

Along the Old 'El':
Southwest Corridor Park

ESSENTIALS		
DISTANCE **3.9** Miles one-way, 7.8 miles round trip	STARTING POINT	Back Bay T Station at Dartmouth St. in Copley Sq.
	TERRAIN	Flat
	LIGHTING	Quite good in most sections
	BATHROOMS	In T stations
	WATER	In select parks along the path
	PUBLIC TRANSPORTATION	Orange line stops along the way
	ADDITIONAL SPURS	Franklin Park, p. 112; Forest Hills Cemetery, p. 120

Overview

Southwest Corridor Park is an often overlooked, great off-road run that starts in the heart of Boston. The 3.9-mile path from Back Bay to the Forest Hills T Station was created in the late 1980s after the Orange Line was put underground some fifteen years earlier. As an interesting bit of trivia, much of this route was going to be an inner I-95 belt cutting through Boston, but activists and Governor Francis Sargent killed the project in the early 1970s. Details on this amazing story can be found at an interpretive sign at the Roxbury Crossing T station along the route.

The trail, also known as the Pierre Lallemant Bike Path, is well-marked in most parts, with separate paths for walkers and bikers in many sections. Starting at the Back Bay T station, at the Neiman Marcus, the first part of the trail winds through the South End, with many small squares, gardens, and parks tended by neighborhood residents. The trail then opens up through Northeastern University, and passes by the new Boston Police Headquarters, the Reggie Lewis Track and Athletic Center, and Roxbury Community College. The final third of the path becomes more neighborhood-ey again, featuring numerous parks, playgrounds, and community gardens. Just beyond the end of the trail is the Forest Hills T Station, marked by its distinctive clock tower. Note that the path is not that well marked in the section between Ruggles Station and Massachusetts Ave. — runners must get onto Camden St. and then the sidewalk along Columbus Ave for a stretch.

This run can be a terrific "there and back", using any one of the several T stops along the way. An option for an ambitious 10-mile loop run, connecting to Jamaica Pond and the Riverway paths, can be found on p. 94. Some excellent additional spurs can be done within ½ mile of the Forest Hills terminus: Franklin Park, the Arnold Arboretum, and Forest Hills Cemetery — all featured separately in this book.

Distance **Directions**

START: Opposite the Back Bay T Station on Dartmouth St, at Neiman Marcus

0.0   Start running "outbound", along path. Notice the pleasant small gardens and parks of the South End.

0.57   **CROSS** Mass. Ave. *Caution: No pedestrian signal.* Northeastern University will be on the left, Carter playground on the right.

       LEFT on Camden St., then **RIGHT** on Columbus Ave., continuing on the sidewalk with Carter playground on your right.

       REJOIN path, just past Northeastern University and its parking lots.

1.27   **CROSS** Ruggles St. (Ruggles T station) (*Caution: tough crossing*) Notice Northeastern University and the Wentworth Institute of Technology.

1.65   **CROSS** Tremont St. Boston Police Headquarters. Just ahead, near the Roxbury Crossing T station, is the Reggie Lewis Track and Athletic Center. There is a terrific interpretive sign at the T station, chronicling the history of the park and the failed attempt at an "inner beltway".

2.31   **CROSS** Center St. (Jackson Sq. T Station)

2.77   Boylston St., Stony Brook T station.

3.23   Green St., with Johnson Playground on the right (basketball courts, ball fields, playground, wading pool). This last section is nicely landscaped, with ball fields, community gardens, and pleasant recreation space.

3.90   **END** at Arborway/Rt. 203, across from the Forest Hills T Station.

       To access the Forest Hills T station, **CROSS UNDER** Msgr. Casey Highway, 0.2 m from intersection with Rt. 203.

7.80   **TOTAL**, with return, retracing route to Back Bay.

SW Corridor Park Segments and Distances

Section	Segment Distance	Total Distance
Back Bay to Mass. Ave.	0.57	0.57
Mass. Ave. to Ruggles St.	0.70	1.27
Ruggles St. to Tremont St./Malcolm X Blvd.	0.38	1.65
Tremont St./Malcolm X Blvd. to Center St.	0.66	2.31
Center St. to Green St.	0.92	3.23
Green St. to Arborway/Rt.203	0.67	3.90
Arborway/Rt.203 to Forest Hills T Station	0.23	4.13

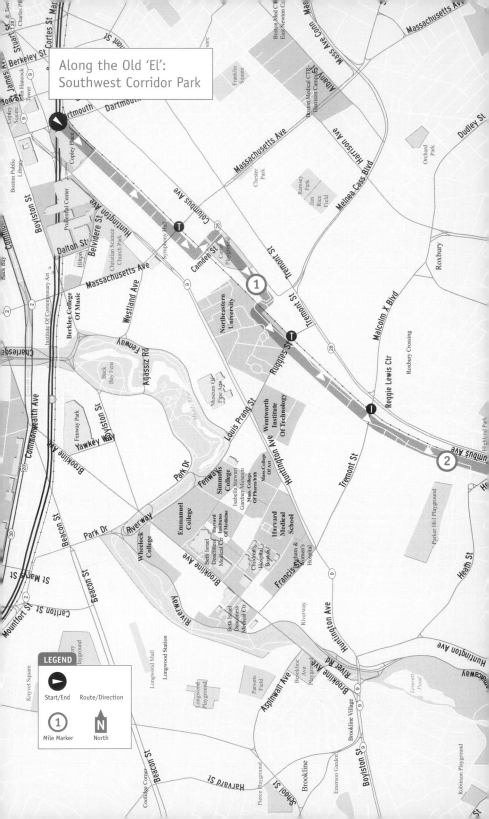

Along the Old 'El':
Southwest Corridor Park

LEGEND

Start/End   Route/Direction

1   N
Mile Marker   North

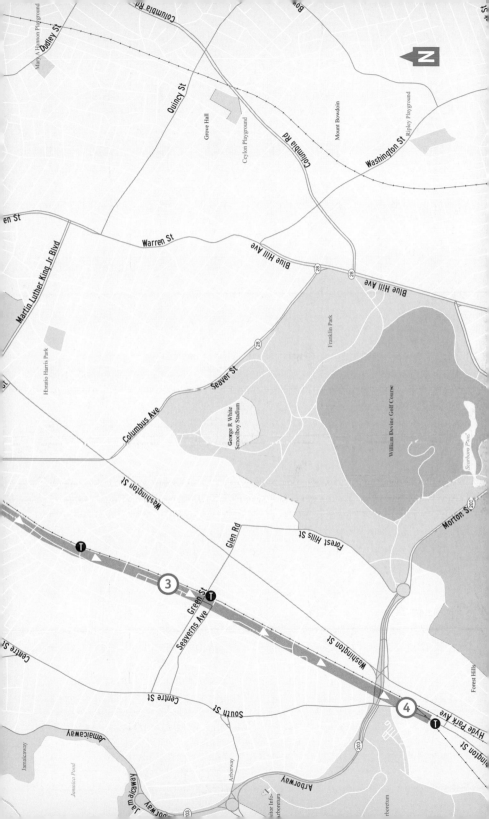

The Grand Loop: Southwest Corridor Park Out, Riverway Path Return

Overview

This run combines a couple of favorites to complete a loop of nearly 10 miles. About 80% of the run is on dedicated walking/running paths, featuring the Southwest Corridor Park path "out", and then looping back through JP, Riverway path, and Commonwealth Ave. Mall for the return. Further descriptive details for this run can be found on p. 90 for the Southwest Corridor, and p. 106 for the Riverway.

The connection through JP is pleasant, passing numerous interesting buildings, shops and restaurants. A Soldiers Monument is at the intersection of South and Center Streets. Eliot Street, which connects the center of JP with Jamaica Pond, is one of JP's oldest streets, featuring the Loring-Greenough House, the Eliot School of Fine Arts, the First Church of Jamaica Plain, and the Footlight Club — the oldest community theater in the nation.

As an option for the return, instead of running through JP to the Riverway Path, you can take the "carriage road" of Rt. 203, called Arborway St., to the rotary at Center St. and then over to Jamaica Pond.

Distance Directions

START: Southwest Corridor Park path entrance, on Dartmouth St., opposite Back Bay T station (Neiman Marcus).

0.0 Start running "outbound", along path. Notice the pleasant small gardens and parks of the South End.

0.57 **CROSS** Mass Ave. *Caution: No pedestrian signal.* Northeastern University will be on the left, Carter playground on the right. *NOTE: Path not well marked between Ruggles Station and Massachusetts Ave.*

LEFT on Camden St., then **RIGHT** on Columbus Ave., continuing on sidewalk with Carter playground on your right.

REJOIN path, just past Northeastern University and its parking lots.

1.27   **CROSS** Ruggles St. (Ruggles T station) (*Caution: tough crossing*)

1.65   **CROSS** Tremont St. Boston Police Headquarters. At the Roxbury Crossing T station is the Reggie Lewis Track and Athletic Center. There is a terrific interpretive sign at the T station, chronicling the history of the park and the failed attempt at an "inner beltway".

2.31   **CROSS** Center St. (Jackson Sq. T Station)

2.77   Boylston St., Stony Brook T station.

3.23   Green St., with Johnson Playground on the right (basketball courts, ball fields, playground, wading pool). This last section is nicely landscaped, with ball fields, community gardens, and pleasant recreation space.

3.90   **END OF PATH**, at Arborway/Rt. 203, across from the Forest Hills T Station.

SHARP RIGHT on Arborway/Rt. 203, briefly, to South St.

RIGHT on South St., to intersection with Center St. at Soldiers Monument.

4.5   **LEFT** on Eliot St. (Tedeschi Food Shop).

FOLLOW Eliot to the end, and the intersection with Pond St./Jamaicaway.

4.85   **CROSS** the Jamaicaway (*CAUTION: Be Careful!!*), onto Jamaica Pond path. Run counterclockwise, passing by the Jamaica Pond boathouse. After about ¾ mile is the intersection with Perkins St. and a crosswalk.

5.6   **EXIT JAMAICA POND PATH** and **CROSS** Perkins St., heading east on the Riverway path, paralleling Pond St., along pleasantly landscaped Olmsted Park. Downs Field will soon be on your left (great 1/4 m track here). Stay on the path, until the intersection with Rt. 9/Riverway/Huntington Ave.

6.4   Facing east, cross Rt. 9/Huntington Ave and continue straight on small road (River Rd., no sign, Brookline Ice Company on left) to the path re-entrance (no sign). Run along path, keeping an eye out for it as you cross Brookline Ave. and Pilgrim Rd. Follow to end (Park Drive, small brick building on left). Fenway T station, REI, Best Buy are across the street.

7.5   **LEFT** on Park Dr. Busy road, but good sidewalk. Continue to Beacon St.

7.7   **RIGHT** on Beacon St. Follow into Kenmore Square, just after crossing the bridge over the Mass. Turnpike.

8.2   At the Kenmore Sq. "T" Station (Green Line), stay on the right (South) side of Commonwealth Ave., crossing Charlesgate and then Mass. Ave.

8.65   **STRAIGHT,** onto the Comm. Ave., onto Comm. Ave. Mall path, just east of Mass. Ave. Continue until reaching Dartmouth St.

9.1   **RIGHT** on Dartmouth St., to end at Back Bay T Station.

9.5   **END**

LEGEND

Start/End   Route/Direction

1 Mile Marker   N North

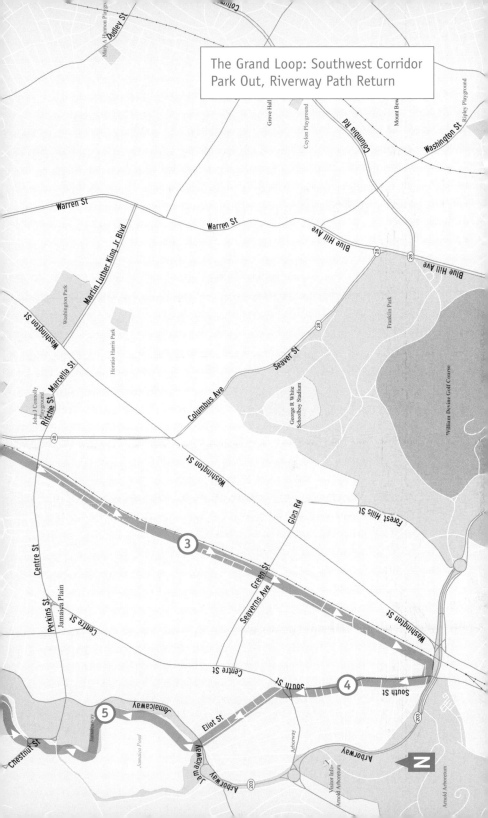

The Grand Loop: Southwest Corridor
Park Out, Riverway Path Return

Ode to Olmsted:
The Full Emerald Necklace
From Boston Common to Franklin Park

ESSENTIALS		
DISTANCE **10.2** Miles **7.5** Miles *(without loop around Franklin Park)*	**STARTING POINT**	State House, top of Boston Common
	TERRAIN	Flat; Most of run is on pathways
	LIGHTING	Most pathway sections not lit at night
	BATHROOMS	Boston Common, Jamaica Pond, Arboretum, Franklin Park
	WATER	Boston Common, Jamaica Pond, Arboretum, Franklin Park
	INTERESTING SITES	The entire Emerald Necklace is an interesting site!

Overview

Boston's Emerald Necklace consists of a 1,100-acre chain of nine parks linked by parkways and waterways. This linear system of parks and parkways was designed by Frederick Law Olmsted to connect the Boston Common, which dates from the colonial period, and the 1837 Public Garden, to the Muddy River and Leverett, Willow, Ward's and Jamaica ponds through the Arnold Arboretum to what was originally referred to as "the great country park" – Franklin Park.

This is an approximately 7-mile route (10 miles if the circuit around Franklin Park is added) one-way, starting at Boston Common and ending at Franklin Park. The run is nearly seamless along lovely off-road trails, although there are a few "connector" sections: between the end of the Commonwealth Ave. Mall and the Fens; Jamaica Pond and the Arnold Arboretum; and between the Arboretum and Franklin Park. Note that this particular run focuses on the main Emerald Necklace route and the connectors. *For additional mileage and to really enjoy some of the gems of the Necklace, please see other runs in this book, referenced in the table on following page.*

Clearly, a "there and back" along the Emerald Necklace, at 14+ miles, is beyond the typical distance of the average recreational runner. There are several options to do parts of this run and return via the "T". The accompanying table has mileage for specific sections, recommendations for "T" returns, and references to other sections in the book for additional description of and runs within Necklace destinations. To do the entire Emerald Necklace one way, to Franklin Park, take the "T" back downtown from the Forest Hills Station (Orange or Green Line) to Back Bay, Downtown Crossing, or Copley Sq.

Distance Directions

START: State House, at top of Boston Common, Beacon St. and Park St.

0.0 **TAKE DIAGONAL PATH**, down Common heading southwest, to light and intersection with Charles St. and the Public Garden.

0.34 **CROSS** the Public Garden, to Washington statue at Arlington St.

CROSS Arlington St., onto Commonwealth Ave. Mall.

1.46 **CROSS** Massachusetts Ave. and continue on the south side of Commonwealth Ave., to Charlesgate West and the complex interchange that crosses over the Mass. Pike.

LEFT on Charlesgate West, crossing over the Pike. Cross busy Boylston St. to the Fens path, heading outbound.

1.88 **ENTER** onto Fens path, at a "Back Bay Fens" sign, running counter-clockwise, with Boylston St. on the right and the Victory Garden on the left.

STAY ON PATH as Boylston St. branches to right. On left, WWII, Korean, and Vietnam war memorials and Kelleher Rose Garden. Park Drive should now be on the left, after Agassiz Rd.

2.13 After Agassiz Rd., stay on path, with Park Drive on the left. After 0.2m, see Roberto Clemente ballfield on the left. There's also a ¼ mile dirt track.

BEAR RIGHT at the intersection of Park Dr. and the Fenway, doing a quick loop around the oval, keeping Park Drive on the right. Just after Peterborough St., at the intersection of Park Dr., the Fenway, and Brookline Ave., **CONTINUE** on path with Park Dr. on the right, to a complex intersection with Brookline Ave., Riverway, Fenway.

CROSS Park Dr., to the beginning of the Riverway path at a small brick building, opposite Landmark Center (REI, Staples).

2.9 **WEST** on path. *(Bike Route sign almost immediately upon entering path)*

3.25 **CONTINUE** on path. Longwood "T station on right.

CROSS Netherlands Rd. (hard to see sign), then Brookline Ave. *Note: The path can be a little hard to track, but stick with it.*

STRAIGHT on River Rd., getting off path briefly. Signage is poor here.

CROSS the major intersection of Rt. 9/Huntington Ave/Brookline Ave., getting back onto path. *See Olmsted Park sign.*

4.0 **FOLLOW** Riverway Path, 0.8 m, paralleling Pond Ave., with Leverett Pond on left, to intersection with Perkins St. (crossing light).

4.8 **CROSS** Perkins St. onto the Jamaica Pond path. The run along the pond path is delightful, with lots of walkers and runners. Run the path counterclockwise around Jamaica Pond, paralleling Perkins St. and then Francis Parkman Dr.

5.4 **EXIT** pond path at intersection of Pond St., Francis Parkman Dr., and Rt. 203/Arborway.

Continued on page 102

State House

LEGEND

Start/End   Route/Direction

① Mile Marker   N North

Ode to Olmsted: The Full
Emerald Necklace

PROCEED ALONG the south side of Rt. 203 East, staying on Rt. 203 at the small rotary, to a gate and entrance to the Arboretum.

5.9   **ENTER** Arboretum at Arborway Gate. Pass Visitor Ctr. on the right, and proceed along Meadow Rd. (no sign) for about 0.5 m.

6.4   **LEFT** at "T", to the Forest Hills gate.

RIGHT onto Forest Hills Rd.

MERGE onto Rt. 203. **GO OVER OVERPASS** to a rotary.

7.2   At rotary, **FOLLOW** Forest Hills Dr. into Franklin Park. The first section is busier.

At another small rotary, **FOLLOW** the main road (map says "Circuit Road" but there is no sign). Soon you will see a pathway next to and paralleling the road, with the golf course on the right.

CONTINUE on Circuit Rd., to the intersection with golf course parking lot.

TURN RIGHT AND RUN THROUGH the parking lot to the other end, passing the club house on the right. At end of parking lot, at a stone marker, continue on the main path (now no vehicles), for the back half of the loop, with the golf course still on the right. Follow back to Forest Hills Drive (no sign, hospital on the left).

EXIT Franklin Park, to a small rotary.

9.7   **WEST** on Rt. 203, on the south side, to Washington St.

10.1   **LEFT** on Washington St. (Java Joe's is a good café/bakery). Follow to Forest Hills T Station.

10.26   **END**, at T Station.

RETURN downtown, on Orange Line or Green Line.

NOTE: If you want to have a shorter run and still cover nearly the entire Necklace, eliminate the loop around Franklin Park. This would save a little over 2 miles.

Emerald Necklace Sections and Distances

Section	Segment Distance	Total Distance
Boston Common to Comm. Ave. Mall	0.5	0.5
Commonwealth Ave. Mall to Fens Path Entrance	1.3	1.8
Fens Path to Riverway Path Entrance @ Park Rd.	1.0	2.9
Riverway Path Entrance to Jamaica Pond	1.9	4.8
Jamaica Pond to Arboretum	1.1	5.9
Arboretum to Franklin Park (rotary)	1.3	7.2
Franklin Park (rotary) into park and Circuit Loop	3.0	10.2

The Fens

ESSENTIALS		
DISTANCE **2.7** Miles	STARTING POINT	Back Bay: Mass. Ave. and Commonwealth Ave.
	TERRAIN	Flat
	LIGHTING	Some sections of path are not well lit.
	BATHROOMS	Kenmore Sq.
	WATER	Fountains in Fens
	INTERESTING SITES	Victory Garden, Kelleher Rose Garden, War Memorial, ball field

Overview

The Back Bay Fens is an interesting transition part of the Emerald Necklace, between the urbanity of the Commonwealth Avenue Mall and the more pastoral Riverway paths connecting to Jamaica Pond and the Arnold Arboretum. The Back Bay Fens has some interesting features. The oldest remaining wartime "Victory Garden" (1941) planted by citizens is today a Community Garden of flowers and vegetables. The World War II, Vietnam and Korean War Memorial can be found tucked behind the Kelleher Rose Garden. There is a playground at Mother's Rest, and the Roberto Clemente ball field, featuring a quarter-mile dirt track around its perimeter. The Fens is also a gateway to the Museum of Fine Arts, the Gardner Museum, and several colleges.

The run starts in the Back Bay at the intersection of Mass. Ave. and Commonwealth Ave. The connection over to the Fens is a bit of a challenge, so please follow the directions carefully! The run around the Fens is about 2 miles, and there are numerous options for add on spurs listed below. I have always found the pathway and roadway layout around the Fens to be a touch confusing, but there are some good landmarks to help in keeping oriented.

Distance Directions

START: Commonwealth Ave. and Massachusetts Ave. intersection.

0.0 **WEST** on the south side of Commonwealth Ave., 0.2 m to intersection with Charlesgate West.

0.2 **LEFT** on Charlesgate West, **CROSSING** over the Mass. Pike. After the bridge, cross over at "Boylston St. Outbound" sign to the Fens path (sign for Back Bay Fens).

0.4 Head **WEST** on the Fens Path, running counterclockwise, with Boylston St. on the right and the Community Garden on the left.

STAY ON PATH as Boylston St. branches to right. Park Drive should now be on the left, after Agassiz Road.

0.65   After Agassiz Road, stay on path, with Park Drive on the left. After 0.2 m, see Roberto Clemente ballfield on the left. There's also a ¼ mile track around the perimeter of the field.

1.0   **BEAR RIGHT** at the intersection of Park Drive and the Fenway. Here you are doing a quick loop around the oval, keeping Park Drive on the right.

1.26   Just after Peterborough St., at the intersection of Park Drive, the Fenway, and Brookline Ave., loop around, and follow the path paralleling "The Fenway".

        FOLLOW the Fenway path, with "The Fenway" road on the right. Simmons College and Emmanuel College are on the right, and soon after that, the Isabella Stuart Gardner museum.

1.7   **STAY ON FENWAY PATH,** passing Museum Road and noticing the Museum of Fine Arts building on the right.

2.1   **CROSS** Agassiz Rd. and stay on the path paralleling the Fenway.

2.4   **REACH** Boylston St. and follow around until reaching the Charlesgate overpass.

        CROSS over the Mass. Pike and return to the start of the run at Mass. Ave. and Commonwealth Ave.

2.7   **END**

Additional Spur Options

- **Running track at Roberto Clemente Field in the Fens.** ¼ mile around.
- **Riverway Path.** This adds an extra 2 miles. You can get onto the Riverway path at the intersection of Park Drive, the Fenway, and Brookline Ave. Cross over this busy intersection to reach the Riverway Path, which starts at a small brick building across the street from Landmark Shopping Center (Best Buy, REI) and Fenway "T" Station. *See the detailed description and map on p. 106.* Follow this route about 1 mile, to the intersection with Rt. 9/ Huntington Ave./Brookline Ave., and return to Park Drive, and then do the "back half" of the Fens run.
- **Commonwealth Ave. Mall.** Follow Commonwealth Ave. east of Massachusetts Ave., to Arlington St. and the entrance to the Public Garden. This adds just short of 1 mile each way.
- **Charles River Paths.** Head north along Mass. Ave. ¼ mile to reach the Charles River paths. There is a ramp heading down to the river path from the Harvard Bridge at Mass. Ave. *See p. 87 for detailed options for the Charles River paths.*

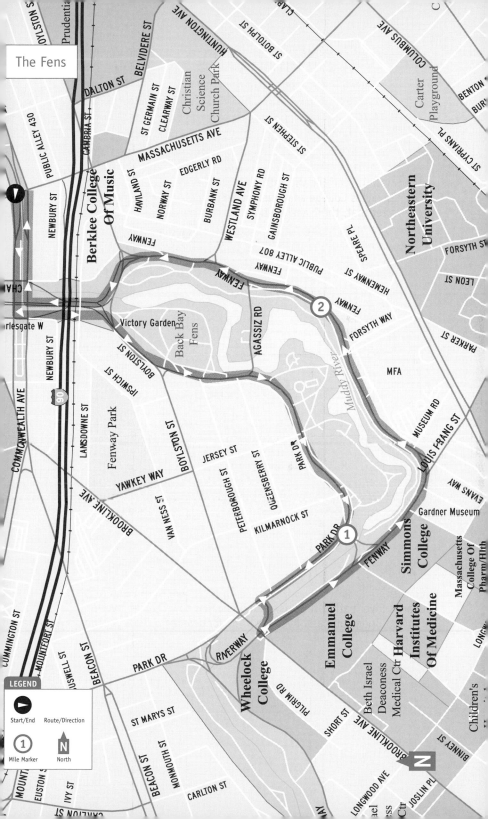

The Fens

Prudential

Christian Science Church Park

Berklee College Of Music

Northeastern University

Carter Playground

MASSACHUSETTS AVE

EDGERLY RD

WESTLAND AVE

FENWAY

Victory Garden

Back Bay Fens

Muddy River

MFA

Fenway Park

Gardner Museum

Simmons College

Massachusetts College Of Pharm/Hlth

Emmanuel College

Harvard Institutes Of Medicine

Beth Israel Deaconess Medical Ctr

Wheelock College

Children's

BOYLSTON ST

NEWBURY ST

DALTON ST

BELVIDERE ST

HUNTINGTON AVE

ST BOTOLPH ST

COLUMBUS AVE

BENTON

BUR

ST CYPRIANS PL

CAMBRIA ST

ST GERMAIN ST

CLEARWAY ST

ST STEPHEN ST

FORSYTH SW

PUBLIC ALLEY 430

NEWBURY ST

HAVILAND ST

NORWAY ST

BURBANK ST

SYMPHONY RD

GAINSBOROUGH ST

PUBLIC ALLEY 807

HEMENWAY ST

SPEARE PL

LEON ST

FENWAY

FENWAY

AGASSIZ RD

FENWAY

FORSYTH WAY

PARKER ST

BOYLSTON ST

IPSWICH ST

MUSEUM RD

LOUIS PRANG ST

EVANS WAY

CHA

rlesgate W

NEWBURY ST

COMMONWEALTH AVE

90

LANSDOWNE ST

BROOKLINE AVE

JERSEY ST

QUEENSBERRY ST

PARK DR

YAWKEY WAY

VAN NESS ST

PETERBOROUGH ST

KILMARNOCK ST

PARK DR

FENWAY

CUMMINGTON ST

MOUNTFORT ST

USWELL ST

BEACON ST

RIVERWAY

PARK DR

PILGRIM RD

SHORT ST

BROOKLINE AVE

LONGW

ST MARYS ST

BINNEY ST

BEACON ST

MONMOUTH ST

CARLTON ST

LONGWOOD AVE

JOSLIN PL

MOUNT

EUSTON ST

IVY ST

CARLTON ST

LEGEND

Start/End

Route/Direction

1
Mile Marker

N
North

Riverway Path and Jamaica Pond Loop

ESSENTIALS

DISTANCE		
5.45 Miles	STARTING POINT	Park Drive, opposite Fenway "T" station.
	TERRAIN	Flat; Mostly pathway. Dirt path around the pond
	LIGHTING	Not lit at night
	BATHROOMS	Jamaica Pond boat house
	WATER	Fountain in front of Jamaica Pond boat house
	INTERESTING SITES	Historic Jamaica Pond, Jamaicaway/Riverway paths
	PUBLIC TRANSPORTATION	Fenway Station; Brookline Village
	PARKING	Ample, on side-streets
	ADDITIONAL SPURS	Track at Downes Field; Fenway Loop, 2.7m, p. 103; Arnold Arboretum, p. 117

Overview

This is one of the loveliest and greenest runs in this book. It is also almost entirely off-road, and incorporates Olmsted Park and the 1.4 mile loop around historic Jamaica Pond. The path along the Riverway is pastoral, crossing over and passing by older stone bridges, passing Leverett Pond and then Willows Pond. In parts there are separate paths for walkers and bikers. There are a couple of confusing sections where the path is not completely seamless, so please read the directions carefully. A good detour is the wonderful track at Downes Field near Jamaica Pond. Good additional spurs are the 2.1 mile Fenway loop (p. 103) and Arnold Arboretum (p. 117).

Distance Directions

START: Park Ave., small brick building across street from Landmark Shopping Center (Best Buy, REI) and Fenway "T" Station.

0.0 **WEST** on path, Bike Route sign just ahead.

0.4 **CONTINUE** on path. Longwood "T station on right.

CROSS Netherlands Rd. (hard to see sign), then Brookline Ave. *Note: The path can be a little hard to track, but stick with it.*

1.0 **STRAIGHT** on River Rd., Brookline Ice Company on the right getting off path briefly. Signage is poor here.

CROSS the major intersection of Rt. 9/Huntington Ave/Brookline Ave., getting back onto path at Olmsted Park sign with Pond St. on the right.

FOLLOW Riverway Path, 0.8 m, paralleling Pond Ave., with Leverett Pond on left, to intersection with Perkins St. (crossing light).

1.9 **CROSS** Perkins St. onto the Jamaica Pond path. Run the delightful 1.45 m counterclockwise around Jamaica Pond, returning to Perkins St. and the traffic light.

3.3 **RIGHT** (heading south) on Perkins St., 0.2 m, to the opposite side of the Riverway path, along the Jamaicaway.

3.5 **LEFT** on path along the Jamaicaway. Pass Willows Pond, Willows Pond Road, a ball field, and eventually Leverett Pond on left. The path will return you to the major intersection of Rt. 9/Huntington Ave./Brookline Ave.

4.3 **CROSS** intersection, onto River Rd. (Brookline Ice Company on left).

FOLLOW path back, repeating the first part of the run.

5.45 **END** at Park Ave. and Riverway/Fenway.

Jamaica Pond, Arnold Arboretum, Franklin Park

ESSENTIALS

DISTANCE **6.8** Miles	**STARTING POINT**	Jamaica Pond, at Arborway (Rt. 203) and Prince St.
	TERRAIN	Some hills in Arboretum; most of run on pathways
	LIGHTING	Not lit at night
	BATHROOMS	Hunnewell Visitor Center in Arnold Arboretum and golf clubhouse in Franklin Park
	WATER	Arboretum Visitor Center; Golf club house parking lot in Franklin Park
	INTERESTING SITES	Jamaica Pond, Arnold Arboretum, many sites within Franklin Park
	PUBLIC TRANSPORTATION	#39 Bus - Perkins Street & Pond Street
	PARKING	Ample parking on Pond St.
	ADDITIONAL SPURS	Riverway path, east of Jamaica Pond, p. 106; Southwest Corridor Park, at Forest Hills Station, p. 90

Overview

This is a spectacular run featuring some of the highlights of the southwestern section of the Emerald Necklace. After starting with a partial loop around historic Jamaica Pond, you will run through the Arnold Arboretum (thereby avoiding running on the rather treacherous Arborway), to green and open Franklin Park, and the 2+ mile perimeter path around Franklin Park. The run is almost entirely off-road, and features a wonderful variety of scenery, from pond views, to the trees and shrubs in the Arboretum, and the open fields of Franklin Park. The only unpleasant section is the 1-mile connector between the Arboretum and Franklin Park. Wouldn't a bike path be nice!

In Franklin Park, there are numerous choices and several interior paths, but a straightforward and pleasant route is the main perimeter road around the park, which also features fine views into fields and the golf course. The first part of Circuit Rd. (marked as such on a map but not in the park) is busier, but there is a separate path next to the road. The back half of the loop is sublime, as it is closed to vehicular traffic.

For the return from Franklin Park to the start of the run, there is an option to use a different route. See the "Loop Option" on page 111.

Start at Perkins St./Parkman Drive at Jamaica Pond

Run on Jamaica Pond path, paralleling Parkman Drive, for about 0.4 m. **EXIT** pond path at intersection of Pond St./Parkman Dr. and Arborway (Rt. 203).

0.4 **FOLLOW** signs for Rt. 203 and Arnold Arboretum, staying on Rt. 203 at the small rotary, to a gate and entrance to the Arboretum.

0.9 **ENTER THROUGH ARBORWAY GATE**, and run along Meadow Rd. inside the Arboretum, for about 0.6m., to a "T".

    LEFT at "T" to Forest Hills gate.

1.52 **RIGHT** onto Forest Hills Rd. **PROCEED OVER** overpass, to a rotary.

2.06 At rotary, **FOLLOW** Forest Hills Dr. into Franklin Park. The first section is busier.

2.31 At another small rotary, **FOLLOW** the main road (map says "Circuit Road" but there is no sign). Soon there's a pathway next to and paralleling the road, with the golf course on your right.

    CONTINUE on Circuit Rd, to the intersection with golf course parking lot.

    TURN RIGHT AND RUN THROUGH the parking lot to the other end, passing the club house on your right. At end of parking lot, at a stone marker, continue on the main path (now no vehicles), for the back half of the loop, golf course still on the right. Follow back to Forest Hills Drive (no sign, hospital on your left).

4.53 **EXIT** Franklin Park, the way you came.

4.76 You are now at the rotary just outside the park.

    RETURN, retracing your steps from the rotary, through the Arboretum to Jamaica Pond.

6.82 **END**

See loop option next page.

Loop Option

Instead of returning the same way, this option provides a different, and pleasant, way to return to Jamaica Pond from Franklin Park, going through the commercial center of Jamaica Plain and avoiding the unpleasant Rt. 203 section. This option is also about ¼ mile shorter than the full return option above.

At Rt. 203 rotary exiting Franklin Park:

Instead of using the overpass, go **UNDER** it, on right hand side, keeping Forest Hills T station on your left. Follow 0.4 m until South St.

RIGHT on South St., and follow about 0.5m to intersection with Center St. You'll see the Jamaica Plain Soldiers Monument, which was erected in 1871 as a tribute to the 23 local men who died in the Civil War. Just ahead is a Tedeschi Food Shop, and Eliot St.

LEFT on Eliot St, passing by same graceful old homes, to end and Jamaica Pond.

CROSS Jamaicaway/Pond St (CAREFUL!!), onto Jamaica Pond path.

Once on Jamaica Pond path, you can return to the start by heading left, clockwise, and retracing the first part of the run. You can also complete the Jamaica Pond loop by turning right, continuing counterclockwise, to the starting point. This would add about a mile to the run.

Add-Ons

- **Franklin Park:** Loop around White Stadium: follow signs in Franklin Park to "Giraffe Lot". Follow paved perimeter road around the field and stadium: about 1 mile.
- **Jamaica Pond:** 1.45m around the perimeter path
- **Numerous add-on path options within Franklin Park,** the Arnold Arboretum, and the Riverway paths. Numerous other runs in this book include those areas.

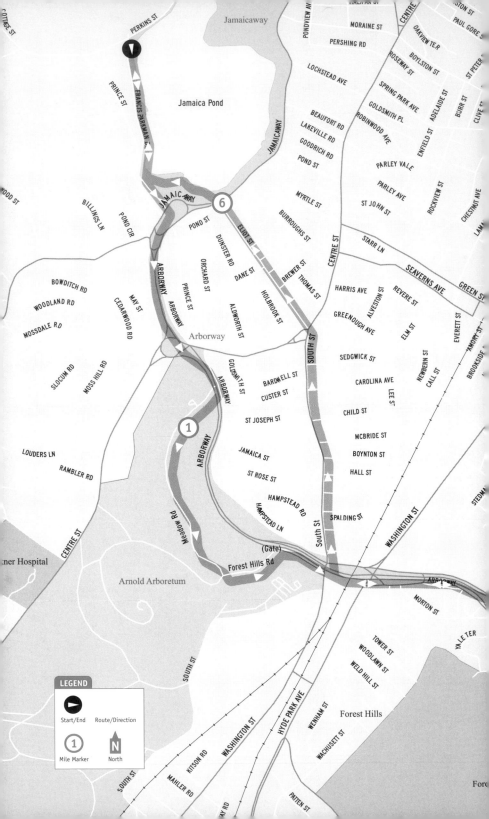

ACADEMY RD

AMORY TER

DIMOCK ST

MARTIN LUTH

WALNUT AVE

CATAWBA ST

RE ST

BRAGDON ST

AMORY ST

ERNST ST

NOTRE

HAZELWOOD ST

ATHERTON ST

W WALNUT PARK

BRAY ST

COBDEN ST

HARRISHOF ST

ELBERT ST

HAROLD

COPLEY ST

WESTMINSTER AVE

HOLWORTHY ST

HUMBOLDT AVE

TOWNSEND ST

YLSTON ST

BEETHOVEN ST

WALNUT PARK

HOLLANDER ST

DECKARD ST

WYOMING ST

DALRYMPLE ST

SCHOOL ST

WALNUT AVE

WAUMBECK ST

MABENO ST

WABON ST

GANNETT ST

GERMANIA ST

WELD AVE

DIXWELL ST

COLUMBUS AVE

CRAWFORD ST

N ST

WASHINGTON ST

CHILCOTT PL

28

HAROLD ST

RUTHVEN ST

HOWLAND ST

WARREN ST

BRUNSWICK ST

HAVERFORD ST

IFFLEY RD

ENNIS RD

BLUE

MONTEBELLO RD

HUMBOLDT AVE

HOMESTEAD ST

CRAWFORD ST

FOREST HILLS ST

PARK LN

WALNUT AVE

PLAYSTEAD RD

SEAVER ST

OLD TRAIL RD

HUTCHINGS ST

GEORGIA ST

PETER PARLEY RD

BROOKLEDGE ST

CHENEY ST

HARTWELL ST

ROBESON ST

George R White
Schoolboy Stadium

ELM HILL AVE

MAPLE ST

SCHUYLER ST

BLUE HILL AVE

SIGOURNEY ST

GLEN RD

PIERPONT RD

WAYNE ST

NAZING ST

SUPPLE RD

PIERPONT RD

GLEN LN

PASADENA RD

28

Franklin Park

JEWISH WAR VETERANS DR

JEWISH VETERANS DR

3

GLEN LN

NORMANDY CT

HEWINS ST

GL

MICHIGAN AVE

WOLCOTT ST

ERIE

OLD RD

ELLINGTON ST

WILLIAM DEVINE GOLF COURSE

BLUE HILL AVE

GLENWAY ST

DAISY RD

JEWISH WAR VETERANS DR

FOWLER ST

PAGE ST

HARLEM

MCLELLAN ST

YOR

CHARLOTTE ST

BRADSHAW ST

JEWISH WAR VETERANS DR

ESMOND ST

BICKNELL ST

GLEASON ST

Scarboro Pond

4

CALDER ST

ABBOT ST

WALES ST

MORTON ST

JEWISH WAR VETERANS DR

ANGELL ST

VESTA RD

N

ST

NIGHTINGALE ST

FRANKLIN HILL AVE

KINGSDALE ST

WILBERT RD

AUSTIN ST

LO

TALBO

BROWNING AVE

Three Historic Greens:
Arnold Arboretum, Forest Hills Cemetery, Franklin Park

ESSENTIALS

DISTANCE		
8.3 Miles	STARTING POINT	Arnold Arboretum, Arborway Gate at Visitor Center
	TERRAIN	Moderately hilly
	LIGHTING	Cemetery closed at night
	BATHROOMS	Visitor Center at the Arboretum; Franklin Park at golf course clubhouse
	WATER	Arboretum; Franklin Park golf course parking lot
	INTERESTING SITES	Flora and fauna of the Arboretum; historic landscaping, memorials, art in Forest Hills Cemetery.
	PARKING	Along Arborway
	ADDITIONAL SPURS	Riverway Path, Jamaica Pond

Overview

This is a unique opportunity to enjoy some of Boston's best green spaces — each of them distinct, beautiful, and historic. This is a run that is nearly entirely on pathways, free of cars, bikers, and traffic. Arnold Arboretum features more than 4,000 different varieties of woody plants and 15,000 trees, shrubs and vines along with world-renowned horticultural collections. Its 265 acres straddle Brookline, Jamaica Plain, and the City of Boston. The terrain, a combination of open meadows, woodland trails, paved and dirt trails, is a delight for running. Franklin Park, at the terminus of the Emerald Necklace, is a beautifully laid out space, with a 2+ mile "circuit" trail around a golf course, with numerous options for additional spurs, including a renowned cross-country course in its interior trails. Not to be missed is Forest Hills Cemetery — Boston's most beautiful and historic rural garden cemetery, featuring more than 250 acres of hills, vistas, winding paths, canopy trees, and fascinating art and sculpture. Established in 1848 and listed on the National Register of Historic Places, the Cemetery was one of Boston's first public parks and was an important influence on Frederick Law Olmsted and the establishment of the Emerald Necklace.

My approach here is to map out the main routes in each location and the best "connectors" between them. Note that the Arboretum section of this run is different in each direction. There are numerous possibilities to add mileage or vary the routes inside each of the Arboretum, Franklin Park, and Forest Hills Cemetery, as well as several options to connect between these three gems.

Distance Directions

START: Arnold Arboretum, Arborway Gate at the Visitor Center

0.0 Follow Meadow Road, 0.6 miles to "T", then left to Forest Hills Gate. At gate, exit onto Forest Hills Rd.

0.6 **RIGHT** on Forest Hills Rd., following Rt. 203 over overpass, to the rotary at Arborway/Rt. 203 and Forest Hills Dr.

1.2 **ENTER** Franklin Park at the rotary, via Forest Hills Dr.

At another small rotary, keep following main road (map says "Circuit Road" but there is no sign). Soon, get onto a side footpath, with the golf course on the right.

Continue on Circuit Rd, to an intersection with the golf course parking lot.

RIGHT, run through the parking lot, passing the club house on your right. At end of parking lot, at a stone marker, continue on the main path (now no vehicles), for the back half of the loop, golf course still on the right. Follow back to Forest Hills Drive (no sign, hospital on the left). On Forest Hill Dr., just prior to main rotary with Rt. 203, see Cemetery Rd./Forest Hills Ave.

3.7 **LEFT** on Forest Hills Ave./Cemetery Rd., going under Rt. 203. Follow Forest Hills Ave. (see signs for the Cemetery) to the Forest Hills Cemetery Gate, up a hill.

4.0 **ENTER** Cemetery through the main gate. Just after the gate, at interpretive area, pick up one of the terrific maps, with provides great detail on the sights of Forest Hills Cemetery.

Inside Forest Hills Cemetery there are numerous options, including many interior trails and paths. This run assumes a full loop around the inside perimeter roads of Forest Hills Cemetery, plus a loop around historic Lake Hibiscus. *Please see the map and detailed run for Forest Hills Cemetery on p. 120.*

This run assumes about 2.5 miles inside Forest Hills Cemetery.

6.7 After completing the Forest Hills Cemetery loop, **FOLLOW** signs near the entrance gate to Tower Street Gate.

EXIT Tower St. Gate onto Tower St., which is a Boston classic of architectural styles.

7.0 **LEFT** on Washington St., to the Forest Hills T Station (Java Joe's café is a good stop). Where Washington St. turns into Hyde Park Ave., **RIGHT** on the connector road, then **RIGHT** on Washington St., to the Arboretum entrance gate at South St. & Washington St.

7.4 **ENTER** Arboretum. Follow South St. to Beech path, connecting to the Bussey Hill Rd./Forest Hill Rd./Meadow Rd. intersection.

7.8 Follow Meadow Rd., between the ponds, back out to Visitor Center.

8.3 **END,** at Arboretum Visitor Center

Three Historic Greens: Arnold Arboretum, Forest Hills Cemetery, Franklin Park

LEGEND

Start/End

Route/Direction

Mile Marker

N North

Arnold Arboretum Run

ESSENTIALS		
DISTANCE *Several Options*	**STARTING POINT**	Hunnewell Visitor Center, Arborway Gate off Rt. 203 near Jamaica Pond
	TERRAIN	Combination of flats and some good hills
	LIGHTING	Not open at night
	BATHROOMS	In Visitor Center
	WATER	In Visitor Center
	INTERESTING SITES	Every season is interesting — there is an incredible variety of trees, plants, and flowers, all beautifully landscaped.
	PUBLIC TRANSPORTATION	Orange Line, Forest Hills; #39 Bus, Forest Hills
	ADDITIONAL SPURS	Jamaica Pond, 0.3m to the path entrance, 1.45m around; Riverway/Jamaicaway paths, p. 106; Franklin Park, p. 114

Overview

The Arnold Arboretum is a true treasure. As the country's first public Arbo retum, it features more than 4,000 different varieties of woody plants and 15,000 trees, shrubs and vines along with world-renowned horticultural col- lections. Its 265 acres straddle Brookline, Jamaica Plain, and the City of Bos- ton, with eight different entrance gates. The terrain, a combination of open meadows, woodland trails, paved and dirt trails, is a delight for running and walking. Good runs of 3-5 miles can be put together by staying within the park boundaries. Boston's highest point is at the top of Peter's Hill, featuring ter- rific views of the city. Note that the signage in the Arboretum is outstanding — there are great maps with "you are here" markers well situated throughout. A detailed guide to the flora and fauna is available at the Visitor Center. Rather than providing a detailed, fixed-route run, I have outlined a few different op- tions. A good map, featuring different loop options, as well as a detailed guide to the trees and plants, is available at the Visitor Center.

Directions

There are eight gates for entering the Arboretum. The runs below all start at the Arborway Gate off Route 203, near Jamaica Pond, which is where the Visitor Center is located.

Route Options in Arnold Arboretum

Route	Distance (m)
Loop 1: Meadow Rd. to Bussey Hill Rd. to Valley Hill Road and Back, adding Willow Path on the way back	3.75
Loop 2: Meadow Road to Linden Path to Bussey Hill Rd. to Valley Rd. to Hemlock Hill Rd. Return along Beech Path to Forest Hills Rd. to Willow Path	3.5
There and Back: Above loops adding, Peters Hill Loop (From Bussey Gate, cross Bussey St. to Peters Hill Gate, left on Peters Hill Rd., around perimeter and back to Peters Hill Gate). Extra 0.4m is up and down Peters Hill. Great views from the top.	4.5
One-Way: Meadow Rd.-Bussey Hill Rd.-Valley Rd.-Hemlock Hill Rd.-Bussey St. Gate	1.5
Add Peters Hill Loop	1.2

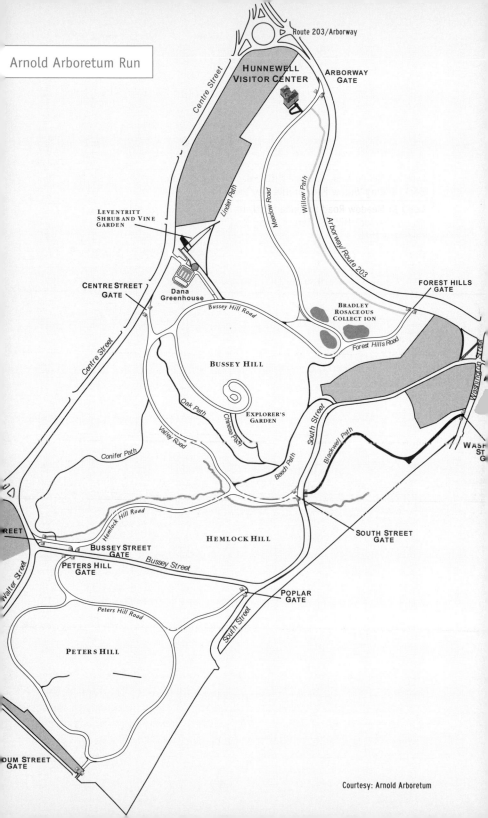

Arnold Arboretum Run

Courtesy: Arnold Arboretum

Forest Hills Cemetery

ESSENTIALS		
DISTANCE *Various Options*	**STARTING POINT**	Main Entrance Gate off Forest Hills Ave. Also a shortcut from the Forest Hills T Station — access Tower St. from Washington St. to the entry gate at the end of Tower St.
	TERRAIN	Gentle rolling hills
	LIGHTING	Not open at night
	BATHROOMS	Entrance Gate building
	WATER	Entrance Gate building
	INTERESTING SITES	Historic landscaping, memorials, public art
	PUBLIC TRANSPORTATION	Forest Hills T Station (Green and Orange Lines); Use Tower St. shortcut from the "T"

NOTE: Forest Hills Cemetery is open 8:30 a.m. to dusk (sometimes gate is open earlier).

Overview

Forest Hills Cemetery is one of Boston's overlooked gems. It is a spectacular venue for walking and running. Even though it is a working cemetery, I have been assured that gentle recreational activities, such as running and even biking, are permitted and even encouraged in the cemetery.

Forest Hills Cemetery is listed on the National Register of Historic Places. Established in 1848, its 250 acres include a variety of terrain, from wood paths to open meadows, a small lake, some great hills — all beautifully landscaped, and featuring specimen trees and unique plantings. There are distinctive, ornamental grave sites to see, and the cemetery is ringed by outdoor sculpture and other contemporary art that has been commissioned over the years. The Forest Hills Educational Trust has done a wonderful job of preserving and celebrating this gem. Every road and path is exquisitely labeled. The Visitor Map and Guide, available just beyond the entry gate, has a detailed map that is very helpful for runners and walkers. It also contains a lot of detail on the horticultural features, a guide to some of the most important monuments, and details on the contemporary art.

Since there are so many meandering roads and pathways, I have not plotted a particular recommended route. I would leave it to individual runners to make their own discovery. It is possible to run for 3-4 miles, covering most of the main perimeter and interior roads and paths. Another recommendation is to combine a run in Forest Hills Cemetery with Franklin Park, which is just across the way (see p. 114 for Franklin Park routes). An entry gate to Arnold Arboretum is also less than ½ mile away.

Some of the highlights of running in Forest Hills Cemetery include:

- Receiving Tomb and Bell Tower at the Main Gate
- Lake Hibiscus. It is about ¼ mile around the perimeter
- Several exotic species of trees along Tupelo Ave. to Dell Ave.
- Grass pathways in the interior of the cemetery
- *Death Stays the Hand of the Sculptor,* a monument by Daniel Chester French, who is best known for the Lincoln Memorial in Washington, D.C.
- Forsyth Chapel, a Gothic Revival Style chapel designed by Van Brunt and Howe
- Pond and Waterfall, off Bell Ave.
- Circle Summit

* Many of the descriptions and highlights are adapted from the Forest Hills Visitor Guide, and are used with permission. Additional information at www.foresthillstrust.org and www.foresthillcemetery.com.

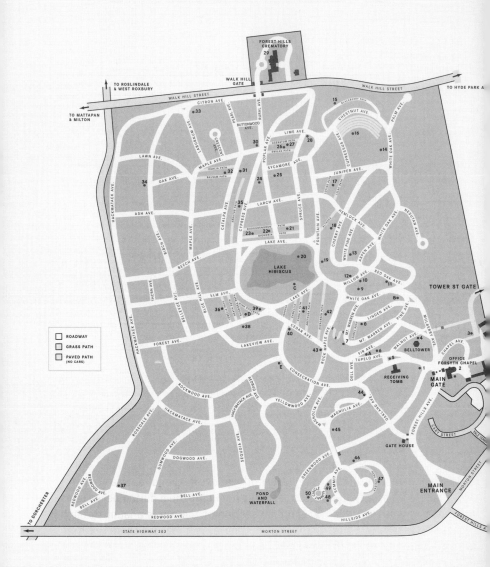

Forest Hills Cemetery

FOREST HILLS CREMATORY
29

WALK HILL GATE

TO ROSLINDALE & WEST ROXBURY

TO MATTAPAN & MILTON

WALK HILL STREET

WALK HILL STREET

TO HYDE PARK A

ROADWAY
GRASS PATH
PAVED PATH (NO CARS)

LAKE HIBISCUS

TOWER ST GATE

BELLTOWER

OFFICE
FORSYTH CHAPEL

RECEIVING TOMB

MAIN GATE

GATE HOUSE

MAIN ENTRANCE

POND AND WATERFALL

TO DORCHESTER

STATE HIGHWAY 203

MORTON STREET

Courtesy: Forest Hills Cem

Historic Parkways:
VFW Parkway and Corey St.

ESSENTIALS		
DISTANCE **6.2** Miles	**STARTING POINT**	Centre St. near VFW Parkway and Bussey St. gate in Arnold Arboretum
	TERRAIN	Flat, except for Corey St.
	LIGHTING	Good
	BATHROOMS	None
	WATER	No public fountains
	INTERESTING SITES	Mt. Benedict and St. Joseph's cemeteries, Hoar Memorial Sanctuary
	PARKING	Along Center St.; side streets
	PUBLIC TRANSPORTATION	No direct subway lines. Bus lines nearby

Overview

A series of roadway connections between parts of the Emerald Necklace was built over 100 years ago. These parkways are maintained by the Massachusetts Dept. of Conservation and Recreation and feature wide, well-kept grassy medians and a lovely tree canopy. While the parkways are principally car thoroughfares, they are surprisingly pleasant for running, featuring sidewalks and good shoulders. Of the parkways accessible from the city, VFW Parkway, originally built to connect the Arnold Arboretum to Stony Brook Reservation, is one of my favorites, typifying some of the most appealing aspects of these old byways. VFW Parkway is listed on the National Register of Historic Places.

This route starts at the Bussey St. gate of the Arnold Arboretum, near the intersection of Central St. and VFW Parkway. There are three main sections of the run. The first is along one of the nicer stretches of VFW Parkway. The run then turns onto Corey Rd., which is a scenic road that bisects Mt. Benedict and St. Joseph's cemeteries, which are beautifully landscaped and feature gorgeous trees that are an especially spectacular sight if you hit them during peak colors in autumn as you crest the hill. The final section of the run is a jaunt through a pleasant section of South Brookline, passing by the Baker School, with an opportunity for a detour into Hoar Memorial Sanctuary, which features 30 acres of pleasant wooded paths (brochure available at brooklinegreenspace.org).

START: Intersection of Center St. and VFW Parkway

0.0 **WEST** on Centre St., briefly, to VFW Parkway.

0.2 **BEAR LEFT** on VFW Parkway at intersection with Centre St. rotary, heading south (toward Dedham). There is a good sidewalk and a grassy median strip. Immediately on your right is Allandale Woods (sign not easy to see), an "urban wild" with a good network of wooded trails.

0.9 At rotary, **CROSS** W. Roxbury Parkway, **CONTINUING** on VFW Parkway another mile, crossing Independence Dr., & Corey St. to LaGrange St.

2.1 **RIGHT** on LaGrange St., briefly, to Brook Farm Rd.

   RIGHT on Brook Farm Rd., to Corey St.

2.5 **LEFT** on Corey St., up and over the hill. There are lovely views at the top of the hill as you run by Mt. Benedict Cemetery. Follow Corey St. to end (LaGrange).

3.1 **RIGHT** on LaGrange St., to Rangely Rd. You are now in South Brookline.

3.5 **RIGHT** on Rangely Rd., following around, crossing Princeton Rd., to Beverly Rd.

3.8 **RIGHT** on Beverly Rd., passing Baker School, to end (Grove St.). *Note: Hoar Memorial Sanctuary, located behind Baker School, makes a nice tour detour, with 30 acres of wooded trails.*

4.3 **CROSS** Grove St., as it turns into Russett Rd.

   STRAIGHT on Russett Rd., returning to VFW Parkway.

4.7 **LEFT** on VFW Parkway, returning to the start of the run.

5.9 **END**

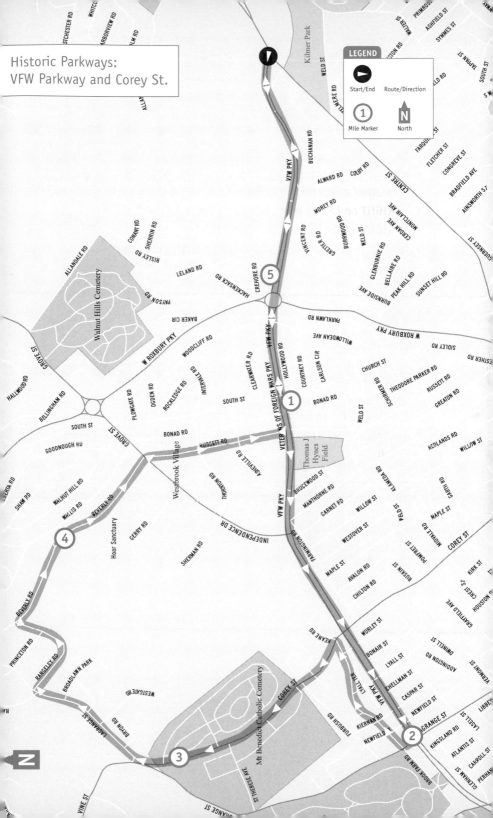

Historic Parkways:
VFW Parkway and Corey St.

Neponset River Greenway

DISTANCE		
6.2 Miles *(3.1 miles each way)*	**STARTING POINT**	North End: Tenean Beach; South end: Central Ave. T Station
	TERRAIN	Flat. Combination of paved and gravel paths.
	LIGHTING	Most of it not lit at night.
	BATHROOMS	Pope John Paul II Park
	WATER	Pope John Paul II Park, Tenean Beach
	INTERESTING SITES	Lovely views to the Neponset River; trolley line along part of path; at northern end, some harbor views; Pope John Paul II Park
	PARKING	Large parking lot at Tenean Beach
	PUBLIC TRANSPORTATION	Central Ave. T near southern terminous of trail
	ADDITIONAL SPURS	HarborWalk to the north, p. 72

Overview

The Neponset River Greenway, opened in 2002, is an approximately 2.5-mile paved biking and walking trail that continues to improve and expand. This is a dedicated path for nearly the entire route, except for a couple of small sections at the northern end along non-trafficked roads. There are some lovely sections of this trail alongside the Neponset River, through parks and playgrounds, benches for resting, and some broader views out to the bay. The trail makes for a pleasant and flat 6-mile round-trip run. It passes through 65-acre Pope John Paul II Park, which, completed in 2001, features its own small network of walking/running paths (perimeter path adds about ½ mile), open fields, nice plantings, picnic tables, and a playground.

Various state agencies and advocacy groups have ambitious plans to connect the Neponset River Trail to other fabulous resources in the area. According to the Boston Natural Areas Network, the master plan is for the completed ten-mile trail to connect eleven urban wilds, through to the 5,800-acre Blue Hills Reservation, and for an improved connection to the HarborWalk.

Distance **Directions**

START: Tenean Beach Park, parking lot.

0.0   The trail starts at the Tenean Beach playground just after Conley St. crosses under the Southeast Expressway. Follow trail, paralleling Tenean St.

0.2   **LEAVE TRAIL** and **TURN LEFT** on Tenean St.

         LEFT on Lawley St.

         RIGHT on Ericsson St.

         RIGHT on Walnut St.

         LEFT on Water St.

         RIGHT on Taylor St.

1.0   **LEFT** on Neponset Trail. From here, you will stay on the trail until its end.

         CROSS Pope John Paul II Park, which is a 65-acre green area with open spaces, walking trails, and water views.

         BEAR RIGHT under Southeast Expressway.

1.5   **CROSS** Hallet St.

2.0   **CROSS** Granite Ave. at light.

         CROSS Neponset River.

         GO UNDER Adams St.

3.1   **END** at Central Ave. T Station (Red Line).

         RETURN along greenway, to Start at Tenean Beach.

6.2   **END**

Additional Spurs:

There are numerous opportunities to add spurs and connect to other runs in this book. Some recommendations:

- **Add spur to Victory Park and Phillips Candy House.** This adds 0.6 miles each way, with lovely water views from Victory Park and an opportunity to sample some sweets at Phillips Candy House, which is Boston's oldest chocolatier, dating to 1925.

- **Connect to South Boston HarborWalk.** It is about 1.6 miles from the northern end of the Neponset Greenway trail to the HarborWalk at UMASS Boston. Unfortunately, about a mile of this connection is along busy Morrissey Blvd., which, while doable, is not especially pleasant for running.

Note: My thanks to Doug Mink, who has detailed this route as part of a longer bike ride.

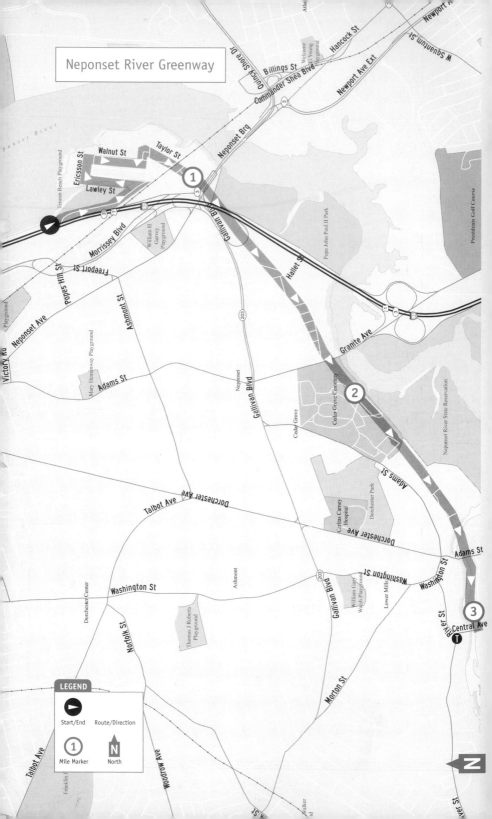

Neponset River Greenway

LEGEND

Start/End

Route/Direction

① Mile Marker

N North